AF618300

Academia Philosophical Studies 50

Rafael Ferber

Key Concepts in Philosophy

An Introduction

2nd, revised and enlarged edition

The Deutsche Nationalbibliothek lists this publication in the Deutsche Nationalbibliografie; detailed bibliographic data are available on the Internet at http://dnb.d-nb.de

ISBN 978-3-89665-942-2 (Print)
978-3-89665-943-9 (ePDF)

British Library Cataloguing-in-Publication Data
A catalogue record for this book is available from the British Library.

ISBN 978-3-89665-942-2 (Print)
978-3-89665-943-9 (ePDF)

Library of Congress Cataloging-in-Publication Data
Ferber, Rafael
Key Concepts in Philosophy
An Introduction
Rafael Ferber
177 pp.
Includes bibliographic references and index.

ISBN 978-3-89665-942-2 (Print)
978-3-89665-943-9 (ePDF)

Onlineversion
Nomos eLibrary

2nd Edition 2021

Visit our website
www.academia-verlag.de

*To be useful as a foundation,
a textbook must contain no more
than the core of a science or art in
the briefest concentration so that
the teacher will easily find cause to
explain the topic concerned.*

Georg Christoph Lichtenberg

Preface

This book is addressed not so much to expert philosophers as to students of philosophy and interested laypersons. It aims to introduce the reader to six key concepts that provide a first understanding of the contents, methods and claims of philosophy. Being an introduction, it is elementary, but not unsophisticated. I try to elucidate those elementary issues clearly, simply and without the use of jargon. At the same time, I do not shrink from adopting a position of my own. My philosophy is indebted in several respects to the analytical school, but its spirit, in a broader sense, is Platonic in so far as it presupposes that the expressions of the concepts under discussion have objective meanings to which we can come nearer, at least to a certain extent. Some new aspects, which could also be of interest to professional philosophers, are found in particular in the chapters about knowledge, truth and the good.

The following people were kind enough to read and make critical comments on selected chapters: Hans Ambühl, Jean Louis Arni, Marcel Zentner. However, I also benefited from the help of the students and non-specialists I have had the privilege of teaching in recent years, and it is to them that I dedicate this book.

Sachseln (Switzerland), autumn of 1993 *R. Ferber*

From the Preface to the English Translation

As a result of its warm reception, the book has now appeared in eight editions, the latest of which also provides the basis for this English translation. As well as a few minor additions, I have included a section about the problem of universals and a reference to the power of judgment. I thank Ladislaus Löb for the translation and Elisabeth Longrigg for looking through most of the book. I wish to thank all those readers who have sent me suggestions for improvement or critical remarks, which I have taken on board as far as I could. I am also grateful to those colleagues who use the book or parts of it in their teaching.

Sachseln, August 2014 *R. Ferber*

Preface to the Second English Edition

For the second edition, I have revised the English translation and made some additions here and there. But I did not change the structure of the book nor its main content, based as they were on the rule to introduce these six key concepts together and limit the main text to authors and contributions that have passed the test of time. It is very easy to find more information on the six key concepts in, for example, the *Stanford Encyclopedia of Philosophy* and other electronic resources. A problem for beginners in philosophy in our digital age is not the lack of information, but the confusing overload of information.
For the revision, I enjoyed the help of Chad Jorgenson and Drew Walker for which I am grateful. I also took into consideration reader critiques. I hope that the present volume will still help students and laypeople to find their way "out of the (digital) cave".

Sachseln, September 2020 *Rafael Ferber*

Contents

I. Philosophy

1. *The Beginning in the Cave*

At one time or another, you have probably sat in front of the television, watching the screen. You saw landscapes, animals, people and products. You probably heard news reports and advertising slogans. Most of the time, you likely assumed that what you were seeing and hearing was real. But was it real? If it was, was it the whole reality? And what does it mean to be real anyway?

I would like to begin with an image. It comes from Plato, the Greek philosopher (427–347 BC). It casts doubt on whether what we see and hear is, in fact, real. According to this image, we humans live in a cave. Since we were children, we have been bound with chains wrapped around our necks and legs. We have been confined in one place and only able to look in one direction. Behind us has been a fire. Running behind our backs, between us and this fire, has been a path. Alongside the path runs a barrier. It is like the screens that entertainers sometimes erect in front of their audiences, behind which they conceal themselves while their puppets perform. These entertainers walk the length of the barrier behind us, between us and the fire, holding up above it all kinds of implements, statues and other images made of stone or wood. Some of the entertainers talk. Others are silent. We, the captives, see only shadows – shadows of ourselves, shadows of each other, shadows of the objects being carried along behind our backs – which are projected by the fire onto the opposite wall of the cave. We take these shadows to be real, and we believe that the voices of those passing by us are the voices of the shadows themselves. Being in such a situation, we fail to see not only the things illuminated by the sun, but even the light itself, be it of the fire or of the sun.[1]

This image is obviously meant to be about us. Plato estranges us from our human situation in order to challenge us to think differently. Most of the time, we live with a sense of false familiarity, not only towards the world, but also towards ourselves. We may, perhaps, be challenged by certain unusual situations that we find ourselves in. But we are not challenged by our common human situation, which does not appear striking

---

1 Cf. R., Book 7, 514a-521 a. The summary refers to 514a-515 a.

to us. The estrangement produced by this odd image disrupts the familiarity acquired by long habit, and we find ourselves in a place where we never thought we could end up – in a cave. And now we are struck. In order to become conscious of the everyday nature of our human situation, we need to appeal to one that is strange. With this in mind, I would like to stress three particular points:

a) We are the captives of images of us, of our neighbours and of those presented to us by entertainers. In Plato's time, these entertainers might have been the poets or the sophists. Today, we could say that these entertainers are the opinion makers whose opinions form our reality.

b) Philosophy is liberation from this captivity of the mind or this captivity by opinions. Since the cave is also an image of the womb, we may further say that philosophy is liberation from the womb of our prejudices. Thus, philosophy is a kind of second birth.

c) Yet, this liberation from the womb also provokes resistance within us. We have an urge to remain there. We are afraid of the pain resulting from such a second birth. Philosophy is not harmless. Sometimes it hurts. It drags us out of the security of our prejudices and takes us to a place where we no longer feel at home. It is almost as if we are transported to another planet. But then, too, the Earth – the cave – appears strange to those who are liberated. Philosophy's liberation allows us to assume the point of view of a stranger. It allows us to see familiar things as if for the first time. In so doing, it takes us out of the human order to which we are accustomed. Thus, philosophy is a kind of death, specifically, the death of a human being ensnared in prejudice. Philosophising also means learning to die,[2] to use a Platonic definition as a metaphor.

The light in virtue of which things are visible outside the cave is that of the sun. What the sun represents in Plato's image is something that we shall still not be able to say at the end of all this. Nevertheless, one thing that this introduction to philosophy may perhaps achieve is to let a ray of light penetrate into the darkness of our cave and, for a brief moment, to set aglow the twilight in which we normally live. This is in fact something that we can reasonably expect from philosophy. The journey from darkness to light has been regarded as the distinctive symbol of philosophy in almost all ages and cultures in which it has existed. Yet, in appreciating this, we still must ask what this symbol means to us.

---

2 Phd., 64a-68 b. For a detailed interpretation of the cave image, see my book, 2nd ed., 1989, pp. 115-148, and Brunschwig, 2003.

2. *Word and Concept*

Let us start with the word "philosophy". It first appears rather late in the history of humankind, that is, about two thousand five hundred years ago, in Greece. It is made up of two Greek words, "*philos*", which means friend, familiar or lover, and "*sophia*", which means wisdom. A philosopher, then, is one who is friendly to or familiar with wisdom. But Plato interpreted "*philos*" as meaning that the philosopher is the friend of wisdom insofar as he does not yet *have* wisdom, but is only *striving* after it. He has Socrates say to the young Phaedrus, in the dialogue of the same title:

> To call somebody wise, Phaedrus, seems to me to be something great and only appropriate to God, but to be a friend of wisdom or something of the kind might be more fitting and more correct in tone.[3]

A friend of wisdom, that is, a philosopher, is in distinction to God only striving after wisdom. Accordingly, philosophy is not a state, but a movement or activity. It seeks to move "from here to there".[4] It is a relationship, like love. It is love of wisdom in a new sense of the word. Wisdom here means neither technical skill nor practical cleverness, but rather knowledge. For, unlike religion, philosophy does not seek merely to *believe* or to have faith, but to *know*. Philosophy is the human urge for knowledge driven to its extreme.

In fact, even Socrates, who did not presume to know much about anything of importance, recognised a difference between knowledge and true belief:

> I think I do not merely guess that true belief and knowledge are different things, but if I were to assert that I know anything at all – which I would not wish to do with regard to many things – I would count this one thing among those that I know.[5]

The difference between knowledge and true belief is that knowledge can supply reasons. Knowledge is "true belief with reason",[6] whereas true belief without reason "falls outside knowledge".[7] For Socrates, philosophy is

---

3 Phdr. 278 d. My translation. An important discussion of the word "philosophy" is found in Burkert, 1960, pp. 159-177, esp. pp. 165-166, and an overview in Moore, cf. esp. Chapter 5, pp. 127-156.

4 Phdr. 250 e. R. 529 a. 619 c. Tht. 176a-b, a basic formula used frequently by Plato.

5 Men. 98 b. My translation.

6 Tht. 201 d. My translation.

7 Tht. 201 d. Transl. Levett.

thus the *activity* of "examining oneself and others" by giving and accepting reasons.[8]

Over the course of the centuries, the word "philosophy" has undergone great changes in meaning. I will highlight only two of these here.

Philosophy in the usual sense – that is, as the word is mainly used today – means a way of thinking or a certain conception. We can speak, for example, of the philosophy of management embraced by a company or the philosophy guiding a country's politics, such as the philosophy of reciprocal deterrence or disarmament. In what follows, I will not use the word in such senses.

In contrast, philosophy proper, in its most authentic sense, means the *doctrine* of first reasons and causes. This definition dates back to Aristotle (384-322 BC).[9] Philosophy, in this sense, is the exploration of principles. For principles are, in fact, reasons. Philosophy is the doctrine of the fundamental reasons accounting for that which is the case.

This brings us to the subject matter of philosophy, which is the world and everything in it. As a medieval thinker once put it: The "religion" peculiar to the philosopher is the study of that which is. Any object may thus potentially become a topic for philosophy: a mouse no less than a man – or nature itself, a painting such as van Gogh's *Sunflowers* no less than a computer. But the philosopher is also interested in concepts such as space and time. Everything knowable belongs to the subject matter of philosophy.

An object becomes a part of the subject matter of philosophy when it is considered from the angle of specific questions. One fundamental question is simply: "What is X?" X here can stand for any object. This question marks the transition from an active attitude to a contemplative or theoretical one. Initially, we adopt an active attitude towards things and humans. We use things, whether they are made by nature or humans. We use a computer, but we do not ask: "What is a computer?" or "What is artificial intelligence?" We may want to have more space, but we do not ask: "What is space?" We ask: "Is there any time left?" but not "What is time?" We may set traps for the mice in the cellar, but we do not ask: "What is it like to be a mouse?" Humans often use other humans as means to achieve their ends, but they do not ask: "What is a human being?" – in contrast, for instance, to a mouse, another animal or even a computer. Normally, we are so confounded by the world that we are simply unable to ask such

8 Plato uses the word for the first time in this new sense in Ap. 28 e.

9 Cf. Metaph. Book 1, Chapter 2, 982b9-10. Revised Oxford Transl.

questions. It is as if, for all the busyness of our lives, we are in a stupor or dreaming in our sleep.

The philosopher, by contrast, is someone who disturbs our slumber. We begin to awaken when we begin to wonder about things or to be astonished by them. Thus, since Plato, the capacity for wonder has been regarded as the beginning of philosophy:

> For this is an experience that is characteristic of a philosopher: this wondering. This is where philosophy begins and nowhere else. And the man who made Iris the child of Thaumas was perhaps no bad genealogist.[10]

Iris is the rainbow, a phenomenon which still fills us with wonder today. The sea god Thaumas, Iris's father, is himself the "wonderous". Aristotle, for his part, confirms this connection: "For it is owing to their wonder that men both now begin and at first began to philosophise."[11]

But what makes the philosopher wonder is not the extraordinary, but rather the ordinary. This is something that generally no longer astonishes people. Just as we no longer notice a sound we always hear, for example, the roar of the surf, so, too, we fail to take notice of what is ordinary because we have become accustomed to it. In the same vein, fish will be the last to become aware of water. But for the philosopher, the "fish out of water", the ordinary is, in fact, the extraordinary, which he tries to explain. He needs no other challenge. Thus, he is, as it were, a "specialist" in what is no longer noticed because of its unspectacular ubiquity. His task is to say what nobody else says, to speak where everybody else is silent. Since what goes unnoticed is usually something quite general, the philosopher's expertise, in contrast to that of the specialist, concerns what is general. Consequently, many of the most important philosophical questions are formed around general notions, such as "what?", "from where?" and "what for?"

Basically, these are the questions asked by children. Some of them have especially aroused the interest of philosophers. Most frequent among these are "what" questions, which can be formulated in the following three- or four-word sentences:

a) What is there? This is the fundamental question of the doctrine of what is to be, the doctrine of being or ontology. For the present, instead of "doctrine of being", we could say "doctrine of reality". Aristotle and many other philosophers right down to our own century have seen the

10 Tht. 155 d. Transl. Levett.

11 Metaph., Book 1, Chapter 2, 982b12-13. Transl. Ross.

question of what is to be as the most fundamental question of philosophy. But since our understanding of the term "being" is inadequate, our answer to this question must first clarify the meaning of the word "being".

b) What do we know? This is the fundamental question of epistemology, given special emphasis by the French philosopher René Descartes (1596-1650). Descartes asks himself whether it is not the case that everything we believe that we know is deception and therefore that our life is like a dream. The purpose of this question is by no means to demonstrate that our life really is a dream. Rather, by means of radical doubt – that is, doubt reaching down to the very roots – Descartes wants to reach what is certain beyond any doubt. The question "What do we know?" then becomes "How can we know anything?"

c) What do we say? This is the fundamental question of the philosophy of language. It applies Descartes' doubts about knowledge to language. Is language only a means of expressing our thoughts? Or can it also steer our thoughts in the wrong direction? If this is possible, the philosopher's first task will be, in the words of Gottlob Frege (1848-1925), "to break the tyranny of the word over the human mind".[12] Ludwig Wittgenstein (1889-1951) is one of the most important thinkers to come to regard knowledge of language as the central topic of philosophy. For him, the question "What do we say?" turns into "What is the meaning of what we say, that is, what is the meaning of a given word?"

d) What is truth? This is the fundamental question of the doctrine of truth. As our understanding of the term "truth" is also inadequate, the doctrine of truth must begin by clarifying the meaning of the term "truth". It must then establish criteria for what we may consider to be true. Since there are likely to be several criteria, the doctrine of truth must, finally, seek to identify the main one.

e) What is good? This is the fundamental question of ethics. Ethics is the doctrine of what is good. Since our understanding of the meaning of the term "good" is, once again, inadequate, ethics must, in the first instance, look into the meaning of the term "good". But the good is something that should be done. Therefore, the question "What is good?" leads to the question "What should we do?"

To put it very simply, the philosophical questions asked in Antiquity and the Middle Ages were primarily about being, those asked in modern times were mainly about knowledge and those asked in the twentieth century

12 Frege, Begriffsschrift, Preface, XII. Transl. Bauer-Mengelberg with modification.

were particularly concerned with language. Philosophical problems, too, have their youth, their prime and sometimes their old age, when they fade back into the background. But sometimes they also undergo a rebirth. Thus, ontological questions have, in our century, once again moved into the foreground. Ethical questions, like questions about truth, have been asked in every epoch in the history of Western philosophy. Other questions are more particular to specific periods.

Naturally, these five "what" questions do not exhaust the list of questions we can ask. At the start of an introduction, we cannot be aware of all philosophical problems, let alone of their possible order of rank. Our awareness of problems also needs time to ripen. Progress in philosophy, therefore, is, at the same time, essentially progress in our awareness of the problems that surround us, but that we do not sense. Therefore, philosophical progress does not consist in the discovery of new empirical facts, nor in the creation of new technologies, whether for making bread or bombs.

Philosophy is not useful in this immediate sense, but neither does it do any harm. When I once asked "What is a philosophical question?", a student replied, with some justification: "A philosophical question is a question where the answer doesn't matter." But man does not live by bread alone, nor is he destroyed by bombs alone. False thinking, too, can contribute to destroying him and his environment. Philosophical progress is progress in thinking and consists in the elaboration and refinement of queries. During this process, we may realise that some questions are formulated incorrectly and we may have to reject them as nonsensical.

But the reason that we are able to ask such questions is not only that we live in the darkness of the cave, but also that we can become aware of this darkness. Occasionally, we glimpse light falling into the darkness. Then we, too, experience something of the liberation depicted in the image of the cave. Then, we become able to count ourselves as belonging to the race that strives from the darkness towards the light.

3. *Philosophy and Common Sense*

Speaking of an "introduction" to the key concepts of philosophy may give rise to the mistaken idea that "we are here – philosophy is there", as if we had been led into philosophy from outside. In reality, we are neither outside of nor indeed above philosophy. We are *in* philosophy, even if we believe that we are outside it. We are introduced to it from within. For we already have a "philosophy" without which we would hardly be able to live, even though we are usually unaware of it. After all, we all have a sound intelligence.

This sound intelligence is also called common sense. According to Immanuel Kant (1724-1804), sound intelligence is nothing more than the average intelligence of a sound human being. Moreover, sometimes the intelligence or common sense of one is the stupidity or nonsense of another. As in the proverb, one person's "owl" is another person's "nightingale".

Nevertheless, our common sense comprises a basic stock of convictions that nobody would be able to abandon without being declared mad. These include personal convictions such as "There is a being that is me". But in addition to a being that is me, there are other people: my father, my mother, my siblings, my wife, my husband, my children, my colleagues and many more, whom I do not even know. I live in a world. This world existed before my birth and it will continue to exist after my death. In addition to the human beings I know and those I do not, there are other creatures, animals and plants that also exist. Despite all the transformations that occurred throughout my life, I am somehow still the same. And like all other living creatures, one day I will no longer be in the world.

Common sense is also philosophical sense. But within this common sense, we all have our own world. It is illuminated by the beam of light deriving from our personal opinions and interests. Whatever falls within this beam is seen clearly. Whatever falls outside it is barely there. Thus, as a rule, for us, most other people hardly exist. Our world is usually a small world. It is, in fact, only a part of the world, which is all that our thought can comprehend, even if we sometimes take it for the whole.

There are philosophers who assert: "[...] whatever we are justified in assuming, when we are not doing philosophy, we are also justified in assuming when we *are* doing philosophy."[13] It is true that we have a basic stock of convictions from which we can scarcely deviate, even in philosophy, without thereby leaving the human community. A poet or composer also expresses feelings that anybody can have, for example, joy or sadness or even a joyful sadness. Likewise, the philosopher can express ideas that anybody may have, for instance, the idea of human ignorance, frailty or transience. At the same time, the thesis of the incorrigibility of common sense would probably serve to detain us in the cave of our prejudices.

If common sense is something "communal", this does not mean that it cannot be questioned. Common sense has, in fact, been able to establish

---

13 Chisholm, Person and Object, Chapter I, p. 16. Emphasis in the original.

"its own facts". Once upon a time, common sense believed, for example, that the Earth was flat, that the sun revolved around the Earth, that about one-fifth of all births were unavoidably accompanied by puerperal fever, and so on. It still believes that the world can be known as it is, however doubtful this notion has continually shown itself to be.

Thus, we all already have a philosophy. We can philosophise only because the seed of philosophy is already within us. But the philosophy of our common sense is not only undeveloped, but sometimes even wrong. What seems to me to be decisive in this context, however, is that we cannot correct this common-sense philosophy from an extra-philosophical standpoint, but only from a philosophical one. We cannot step out of philosophy to look at it from the outside and to adopt a standpoint that would supply us with a yardstick for judging what is right and what is wrong with our everyday philosophy. Rather, common sense must create this yardstick – and, in essence, extract the elements for self-correction – from itself. This process has been aptly described as follows: "We are like sailors who must rebuild their boat on the open sea, without ever being able to put into dock and reconstruct it from the best components."[14]

Just as there is no standpoint outside language from which we can speak about language, there is no standpoint outside philosophy from which we can philosophise about philosophy. The practical consequence of the impossibility of a philosophical standpoint existing outside philosophy is the inevitability of philosophising. Aristotle expresses this situation by means of the following dilemma: We must either philosophise or not philosophise. In order to prove that we must not philosophise, we must philosophise. Therefore, we must philosophise even when we argue that we must not philosophise.[15]

4. Philosophy, Science and Art

But has philosophy not long since been replaced by the sciences? At its origin, among the pre-Platonics, philosophy could not be separated from science, but today, one might think, the sciences have caught up with and indeed overtaken philosophy. Now philosophy is only required to address

---

14 Neurath, 1932-1933, p. 206. Transl. Schlick. The image has become famous as the motto adopted by Quine, Word and Object, VII.

15 The dilemma is handed down to us in several versions. Cf. Protrepticus, p. 44, fragments A3-A6. My paraphrase.

the residual problems of the sciences, until these residual problems, too, are completely taken over by the sciences. Proponents of this opinion can rightly point out that individual disciplines, such as physics, psychology, mathematics and others, have broken loose from philosophy, and that the process of differentiation into special disciplines continues. Philosophy, the daughter of Thaumas the "wonderous", has become the mother of many sciences. Thus, formal logic, for example, was originally part of philosophy, but today, in its mathematical form, it is increasingly establishing itself as a discipline in its own right, which once again is breaking down into sub-disciplines.

However, the claim that the sciences can replace philosophy may be countered by the following consideration: New sciences also create new philosophical problems. Formal logic in its mathematical form led to the philosophy of mathematical logic, informatics to problems of artificial intelligence, and biotechnology to ethical problems, such as whether we may morally do what we are technically able to. Although the same questions are asked time and again, the range of philosophical problems does not remain the same. Scientific progress also creates new philosophical problems. To the extent that the new sciences address these new, self-created problems, we may talk about the "philosophification" of the sciences. Thus, philosophy has not moved out of the campus buildings representing the many sciences, but has rather moved into them.

At the same time, many of the individual sciences are unable to access many philosophical problems. Thus, none of the individual sciences asks what it actually means *that something "is"*. Rather, they assume that something is, without explaining the meaning of this "is". Nor do they normally ask general questions, such as "What is knowledge?", "What is language?", "What is truth?", "What is good?" The sciences claim to be paths to the truth, but they do not ask "What is truth?" By contrast, where the sciences do ask such questions and try to answer them methodically, they begin to be philosophical. The limited range of the sciences, then, is another reason we cannot say that philosophy has been replaced by the individual sciences. But without doubt, parts of philosophy have been taken over by the individual sciences. This process of the scientification of originally philosophical disciplines will continue.

But is philosophy a science at all? Several philosophers have believed that philosophy is related not so much to science as to poetry. Accordingly, they expressed themselves in a figurative, rather than a conceptual language. In this context, we could mention Plato, along with some of his dialogues, for instance, the *Phaedrus*; St Augustine (354-430), with his *Confes-*

sions; Friedrich Nietzsche (1844-1900), with *Thus Spoke Zarathustra*; and others. There is a sense in which these thinkers produced philosophy poetically. Today we can observe again that some philosophers are trying to speak like poets.

Conversely, we also find an increasing "philosophification" of the arts today. This is how the French poet Saint-John Perse put it in his Nobel Prize address: "Since even the philosophers are deserting the threshold of metaphysics, it is the poet's task to retrieve metaphysics; thus poetry, not philosophy, reveals itself as the true 'daughter of the wonderous', according to the words of that ancient philosopher to whom poetry was most suspect."[16]

The ancient philosopher in question is Plato, who ushered the poets from his ideal state. I would like to name two such philosophical works of art: first, Samuel Beckett's *Waiting for Godot*. In this play, two men, Vladimir and Estragon, are waiting for a Mr Godot, who is expected to come, but never does. Godot is an allusion to God, or at least an important unknown person. *Waiting for Godot* can be regarded as a symbol of a life spent waiting for an event that does not take place. Another example is the film *Stranger Than Paradise* by Jim Jarmusch. Two men are travelling aimlessly from New York through America and end up in Florida, which may symbolise paradise. One of them falls in love with his cousin, whom he has met at the home of his Hungarian aunt and taken to Florida. When the cousin tries to leave for Budapest without warning, he decides on the spur of the moment to follow her. But she misses the plane and stays in Florida, while he catches it and ends up flying to Budapest. It is not easy to put into words the philosophy that is shown, but not articulated, by the film. But it does show the meaninglessness, randomness and unpredictability of real life, which is even less familiar to us than the paradise we dream of.

Nevertheless, the majority of philosophers have stressed the scientific character of philosophy. One of these is, once again, Plato, with his dialectic, even though it is never fully developed in the dialogues. Plato understood dialectic to be a science, which, by means of elaborate conversation, tries to discover what everything is. Other such philosophers include Aristotle, with his *Metaphysics*, that is, the "theoretical science of first causes and principles";[17] Descartes, with his *Principles of Philosophy*, which tries to anchor the unshakeable first principle of philosophy in consciousness; and, not least, Kant, with his *Prolegomena to Any Future Metaphysics That Will Be*

16 Saint-John Perse, 1972, p. 444. Transl. Auden with modification.

17 Cf. Metaph., Book 1, Chapter 2, 982b9-10. Revised Oxford Transl.

Able to Present Itself as Science. In the twentieth century, it was above all Edmund Husserl (1859-1938), with his programmatic "Philosophy as Rigorous Science" (1911), and Rudolf Carnap (1891-1970), with *The Logical Structure of the World*, who tried to develop a scientific philosophy and, in so doing, laid the foundations for philosophical trends that are still influential today. For these thinkers, "scientific" means logically compelling to anybody who is able to follow the train of thought. All those who set out with the same basic assumptions are bound to arrive, by means of step-by-step deductions, at the same conclusions, such that there is no room left for personal opinion. It is no coincidence that Kant wrote his main work, *Critique of Pure Reason*, under the motto "About ourselves we keep silent" and dispensed with an autobiography. For it is not the person, but only the work, that counts. It must be said, however, that this dream of a scientific philosophy, to which all human beings are committed, has never been fully realised.

Not only are the basic assumptions of almost all philosophers open to some kind of challenge and the basic terms in use generally ill-defined, but the conceptual analyses and derivations also usually leave much to be desired. The elimination of all personal opinion seems to be as impossible in philosophy as the elimination of all error. It is true that even in the most exact natural sciences – mathematical physics, for example – there is no absolute knowledge that is valid for all time. All of the laws of physics that are valid today could be proven false tomorrow (cf. p. 49). But while in physics there is a degree of agreement about which laws are valid, the disagreement about the principles of philosophy that has existed ever since the pre-Platonics will continue, albeit at a different conceptual level. The idea of converting this fundamental dissent in philosophy into a consensus through a process of scientification will probably always remain a mirage. For philosophy – that is, human striving after knowledge – seems to contain within itself a demand that successfully resists scientification.

At the same time, drawing a clear dividing line between science and art, or between subjective and objective, is hardly feasible. Rather, philosophy has proved to be so malleable that any attempt to define it too narrowly would be inappropriate. Just as philosophy itself has no sharp boundaries separating it from "non-philosophy", there are also no sharp boundaries between philosophy, science and art. Even on the formal level, a certain diversity is a characteristic of philosophy. A purely scientific or purely subjective philosophy has probably never existed, but there are different degrees of subjectivity and objectivity. The classical philosophers of the past and the present spent their lives looking for objective truth, but were only able to express it in their subjective ways. Since they did this well and each in his own unmistakable style, most of the significant works of philosophy, from Plato's *Republic* to Wittgenstein's *Philosophical Investigations*, are also works of literature: Their form and content cannot be separated out, but rather the literary form is part of the content.

Thus, the narrative framework of a Platonic dialogue can tell us various things about the content of that dialogue. That Socrates, in the *Republic*, walks from the Piraeus to Athens may indicate that philosophy is an ascent. A great philosophical work, as it were, leaves nothing to chance and, like a good Platonic dialogue, takes no step in vain. Great philosophy, therefore, does not preclude, but actually includes, the structured expression of a great human being: "The greater the man, the truer his philosophy."[18] "Truer" is probably used here in the figurative sense of more significant and richer. Conversely, one Platonist was not ashamed to confess his uncertainty:

> But we can all make it our purpose that our philosophy, if we have one, shall be no mere affair of surface opinions, but the genuine expression of a whole personality. Because I can never feel that Hume's own philosophy was that, I have to own to a haunting uncertainty whether Hume was really a great philosopher, or only a "very clever man".[19]

5. Philosophy as an Ideal

The terms "philosopher" and "philosophy" have not only a descriptive meaning, but also a judgmental one. Like knowledge of the objective truth, philosophy is also an ideal that has been approached, but never fully realised. The reason for this, in addition to human frailty, is the difficulty of the questions asked by philosophy. We may be surprised to discover that we can live without having solved even those philosophical questions that affect us personally. Levin in Leo Tolstoy's novel *Anna Karenina* was probably not alone in experiencing some painful moments because he found no answers to questions such as these:

18 Spengler, DW, Introduction, Section 15, p. 41. Transl. Atkinson.
19 Taylor, Hume and the Miraculous, p. 365.

> Without knowing what I am and why I'm here, it is impossible for me to live. And I cannot know that, therefore I cannot live.[20]

Once we have started to solve philosophical questions, sooner or later we feel that we are not up to solving them completely. Yet, we must live and philosophise, or at least try to do so, for the most important questions human beings can ask themselves are philosophical questions. Moreover, the human mind has an ineradicable tendency to ask these questions. "All men by nature", Aristotle says, "desire to know".[21] All men, one might also say, by nature desire philosophy. For the human mind is by nature philosophical. Philosophy is the fulfilment of this striving for knowledge, which, however, most of the time only exists as a possibility and is often hampered and misled in its development.

"Music unfolds me", Goethe is supposed to have said. Philosophy does something similar. It unfolds our understanding of key concepts. What makes philosophy more difficult is that this unfolding encounters not only external obstacles, but internal ones as well. These obstacles lie essentially in the cognitive "weakness of the *logoi*",[22] that is, the narratives and arguments, with which we try to unfold these concepts. These do not give us immediate access to the "truth of things",[23] but use "somehow or other"[24] our own cognitive instruments, such as names, definitions, images and concepts. Our cognitive instruments often do not deliver to us the essence we seek, but only "properties", "appearances" or "aspects" of this essence. They reveal this essence as it reveals itself from their perspective. Therefore, as much as we seek what being, knowledge, language, truth or good "really" are, as little do we finally find *what* they "really" are. We find their essence only in the way that it reveals itself from the perspective of our cognitive instruments.

The philosopher seems destined not to find what he seeks. His soul seeks "the what" or the essence.[25] This search is, as it were, implanted in a philosophical soul and serves perhaps even the interest of most of his fellow human beings. Thus, Plato has Socrates ask: "Or don't you believe it to be for the common good, or for that of most humans that the real nature of each

---

20 Anna Karenina, Part 8, Chapter 9. Transl. Richard Prevear and Larissa Volokhonsky.

21 Metaph., Book 1, Chapter 2, 982b9-10. Transl. Ross, rev. Barnes.

22 Plato, Ep, VII 343 a.

23 Plato, Phd. 99 e.

24 Plato, Ep. VII 342 e.

25 Cf. Plato, Ep. VII 343b-c and my interpretation, 2007, pp. 65-66, 94-121.

existing thing should become clear?"[26] Similarly, Aristotle writes: "And we believe that we know most about all things if, instead of their quality, size or location, we know what is man, or fire."[27] Even if we deny that there is such a thing as essence, we nonetheless implicitly assume that there is an essence. Even if, like Wittgenstein, we do not accept an essence of language, but only a "family resemblance" between languages,[28] we nonetheless still assume that there is an essence of language. "Family resemblance" signifies the common features and differences between family members: Applied to languages, it signifies the presence of common features, despite the differences between languages. But to assume necessary features common to languages is to assume that there is an essence at least of human language.[29]

Yet, the cognitive instruments themselves present to the soul time and again only what it does not seek, that is, not the essence, but only "properties", "appearances" or "aspects" of this essence, for example, "family resemblances". The philosopher trying to make headway in the struggle with a problem seems destined for defeat. This had been put somewhat dramatically as follows: "He is always striding towards defeat and even before joining the battle he bears the wound in his temple."[30] The same experience, but with a more positive outcome, is conveyed by Rainer Maria Rilke in a poem called "The Walk":

> So does, what we were unable to grasp, grasp us, full of appearance,
> [...] and transform us, even if we fail to reach it.

---

26 Chrm. 166 d. Transl. Sprague with modification.
27 Metaph., Book 7, Chapter 1, 1028a36-b1. Transl. Ross with modification.
28 Cf. in particular PI § 63-67. Transl. Anscombe.
29 Cf. e.g. the detailed critique of Wittgenstein's conception of family likeness in PI, § 63-67, by Holenstein, Sprachliche Universalien, pp. 169-210.
30 Ortega y Gasset, 1983, p. 434.

II. Language

1. Speech as Action

Let us begin with language. At this early stage, we are not yet ready to begin with a direct enquiry into being or knowledge. Methodologically speaking, it is more appropriate to begin by revisiting the instrument that we use to philosophise about being or knowledge, an instrument we call language. Although language is an indispensable instrument of philosophy, it is nevertheless difficult to describe it. Since we are almost always using language, it is something very close to us. When we talk about language, it is almost as if we were talking about ourselves and, while it is difficult to talk about ourselves in an appropriate manner, it is just as difficult to talk about language in an appropriate manner.
On this note, an aphorism of Georg Christoph Lichtenberg tells us:

> Words are a kind of mathematics in letters for the natural signs of the concepts which consist in gestures and postures, the cases of nouns are the signs.[1]

The natural signs of concepts, then, are not words, but gestures and postures. Words are only abbreviations for these natural signs. Language, at its origin, is not spoken language, but rather body language. Of course, spoken language also uses different parts of the body, such as the larynx and the mouth. To this extent, spoken language, too, could be called body language. We do, in fact, use our larynx and our mouth for speaking, as a result of the development of the human species from other forms of life, that is, as a result of evolution.
Evolution could also have taken a different course. For instance, we could have developed the ability to talk with our hands or feet or stomach, although this would have made communicating complicated issues more difficult. But the fact that speech was originally an activity of the body, and spoken language, as it were, a mere extension of this activity, has important consequences. Like the movement of our body parts – such as our hands and feet – using our speech organs is an action. Just as we perform

1 Lichtenberg, Aphorismen, Sudelbücher, Booklet A, § 103. Not found in the translation of Hollingdale.

bodily acts when we walk, run, wave and greet someone, so, too, do we perform verbal acts when we speak. Thus, Socrates is right when he says that "speaking is a kind of action".[2]

This becomes even clearer if we compare language with a game, say the game of chess. Just as we perform various actions when we move the chess pieces, so, too, do we perform actions when we use words. In this regard, Wittgenstein introduces the concept of linguistic action as follows: "For us language is a calculus; it is characterised by *linguistic activities*."[3] What he means by it being "a calculus" becomes clearer if we think of language as a "kind of mathematics in letters" or a game of chess. In chess, we have various pieces: the king, the queen, the rook, etc. Their functions are defined by the rules we follow in playing with them. Like using chess pieces, we have a multiplicity of words in language, whose functions are determined by the rules we follow in using them. Language, then, can be described as calculus, insofar as it is a system of linguistic terms working together with the rules governing the corresponding actions. Wittgenstein calls "the whole of language and all the activities with which it is interwoven the 'language game'".[4]

But since language is rooted in speech, it has become customary to refer, not to linguistic activities, but to "speech acts". John Searle, for example, wrote a book with the title *Speech Acts* which also connotes the verb form: "Speech *acts*".[5] A speech act is the production of a linguistic expression according to specific rules.[6]

Just as we perform body acts in different ways and for different purposes, so, too, can speech acts be of different kinds and serve different purposes. In his book *Philosophical Investigations*, Wittgenstein makes a list of such speech acts, in which he includes:

> Giving orders, and acting on orders.– Describing the appearance of an object, or giving its measurements – Constructing an object from a description (a drawing) – Reporting an event – Speculating about an event – Forming and testing a hypothesis – Presenting the results of an experiment in tables and diagrams – Making up a story; and reading it – Play-acting – Singing catches – Guessing riddles – Making a joke; telling it – Solving a problem in practical arithmetic – Translating

---

2 Plato, Crat. 387 b. My translation.
3 Wittgenstein, PG, Part 1, Chapter 10, § 140, p. 193. Transl. Kenny.
4 Wittgenstein, PI, § 7. Transl. Anscombe.
5 Searle, Making the Social World, chapter 8, p. 190.
6 Cf. Searle, Speech Acts, Part 1, Chapter 1, Section 4, p. 16.

from one language into another – Asking, thanking, cursing, greeting, praying.[7]

2. *Three Functions of Linguistic Action*

Just as life continues to evolve, so, too, can new speech functions – that is, new objectives for speech – develop, while others die off. I would like to highlight here three of these that occur particularly often: the descriptive function, the expressive function and the directive function.

By the descriptive function of language, we mean the construction of true or false sentences that convey true, false or merely probable information. We see this language function at work in particular in weather forecasts, stock exchange reports, reports about traffic conditions, etc.

The expressive function is found in exclamations such as "Wow", "Ouch", "Oh" or "Hey". But it is also prevalent in poems, for instance in the following lines: "Roses, godknowshow so beautiful, / the city in green skies / in the evening / in the transience of the years!"

Nobody will accuse the poet Gottfried Benn here of peddling false information because he calls the evening sky green. The question of truth or falsity is clearly of secondary importance to the melancholy tinged with hope that overwhelms the aging poet at the sight of the roses. This expressive function, however, is by no means restricted to merely expressing feelings. It can also arouse feelings, just as the crying of a child, woman or man can serve either to express or to evoke feelings.

Finally, the directive function occurs in such commands as "Look out!" or "Stop!" and in requests such as "Please rise".

It is important to note that these three central linguistic functions rarely appear in their pure forms. Poems also very often convey information, and scientific reports often contain exclamations and value judgments which seem to be phrased objectively, but which are not always objective. This fact led one famous critic to the observation that in such writing, "they talk about the matter in hand, but they mean themselves" (Karl Kraus).

The directive language function also rarely appears in isolation, except, perhaps, when used in the armed forces or in speaking to children and animals. As a rule, adults cannot simply be given orders. Nor is it enough to issue a cheque bearing the words "For the poor". It is necessary to give further information about the nature of their poverty and the purpose of the

---

7 Wittgenstein, PI, § 23. Transl. Anscombe.

gift in order to show that one does not intend merely to exploit the donor's generosity, but to spend the money sensibly. But even if there can be no doubt that the money will be used for a constructive purpose, it is still necessary to evoke positive feelings with respect to that purpose. In order to evoke feelings, then, the expressive language function is also needed. Such varying uses and requirements of language, just described above, show that the three different language functions are by no means separate. Effective communication uses all three functions in tandem.

These three language functions seem to correspond to three different grammatical forms. The descriptive function occurs mainly in declarative sentences, the expressive in exclamative sentences and the directive in imperative sentences. It may therefore seem possible to infer the function of an utterance directly from its grammatical form. Yet, this is not, in fact, the case. Just as the same smile can be ambiguous and suggest, for example, affection, irony or *schadenfreude*, so, too, can one and the same speech act perform a range of functions. The declarative sentence "That was very nice", uttered after a lecture, can express the feeling that the lecture was very good. Uttered by a host after an enjoyable evening, it can communicate an invitation to the guests to come again, while – under the right circumstances – it can also serve as a hint designed to make the guests take their leave. Many poems and prayers are dressed up as declarative sentences, but primarily express a feeling. The psalmist writes: "Thou shalt tread upon the lion and adder; the young lion and the dragon shalt thou trample under feet."[8]

With these verses, the psalmist is not transmitting certain information, but trying to express a sense of certainty. An order can be clothed in the form of an interrogative or an optative sentence. Instead of "Bring me a coffee!", we can say "Could I have a coffee?" Politeness actually bids us to do this. An exclamation such as "It's very nice here!" can have a directive function, for instance, by inducing a person to stay in a given place. All of this goes to show that although grammatical form often indicates function, there is no necessary connection between the two.

Beyond grammatical form, there is actually no necessary connection between content and function. When we talk about the weather, we are not, as a rule, aiming to deliver a weather report. Rather, we want to start a conversation or simply just to say something. As Oscar Wilde put it: "Whenever people talk about the weather I always feel quite certain that they mean something else."

8 Psalm, XCI 13. Transl. King James Bible.

It is possible to say "yes" and to mean "no", or vice versa. In a letter, we sometimes have to read not only the lines themselves, but also between the lines. In a Platonic dialogue, for example, when Socrates asks a question about a trifle, this trifle is actually the most important thing. Another example would be irony. When we speak ironically, we mean just the opposite of what we are saying. It would sometimes seem as if humans have been given language in order to conceal, instead of reveal, their thoughts. Louis Armstrong sings: "I see friends shaking hands, saying how do you do. They are really saying, I love you."
The crux of the matter is that there is no mechanical method that would allow us to infer the function of a sentence from its form (or its content). In order to do so, we must try to interpret the meaning of the individual acts of speech or writing, which can only be learnt through experience and reflection. This interpretation alone will tell us what particular speech acts mean.[9]

3. *Expression and Meaning*

But how do we get from the mere form of an expression to its meaning? The meaning does not manifest itself as something separate from the expression. When we hear a person utter a word or a sentence, we not only hear a noise, but we also become aware of a particular content. When we read a book title or a headline, we not only make out letters, but we also identify a topic. When we read the word "beware", we do not simply scan the letters b, e, w, etc., but we also grasp a warning. When we unexpectedly come across a sign saying "Beware of falling rocks", we may experience a slight shock. When we are fretting over a delayed train and we suddenly catch a glimpse of a poster with the slogan "Let the train today take the strain away", we may burst into laughter. In all of these cases, we not only see letters or hear sounds, but we also recognise a particular content. By "word", we usually mean both the physical event – a bundle of sound waves or scribbles on paper – and its corresponding meaning. Likewise, by "sentence", we usually mean both the physical event and its corresponding meaning.
For what it is worth, this is how we perceive spoken and written language directly. What we perceive directly is also what philosophers call "appearance" or "phenomenon". "Phenomenon" comes from the Greek

9 I am indebted here to Copi, Introduction to Logic, Chapter 2, pp. 68-71.

phainómenon, meaning "that which appears". In phenomenology, that is, the doctrine of appearances, founded by Edmund Husserl and carried further by Martin Heidegger, it becomes a technical term referring to a specific method for contemplating objects. The key feature in this method is that it tries to dispense with all prior knowledge and seeks to perceive objects as they present themselves in their own essence. Only an object seen in this light can be called a phenomenon in the phenomenological sense of the term. Heidegger defines a phenomenon as "the entity's showing itself in itself".[10] However, because what shows itself through itself is often hidden by our preconceived notions, we can refer to the revelation of what is given to our perception directly as "phenomenological description".

This revelation we call phenomenological description can be resolved into its more basic elements. To resolve something is to analyse it. To analyse comes from the Greek *analýō*, which means "I resolve". When we analyse, or resolve, phenomenological description into its elements, we must distinguish between the expression, or, rather, the *form* of expression or "sign-design", and its meaning. The expression is the single occurrence of a word, while the form of expression or sign-design is the recurrent shape of this word. The expression "Attention" is the single occurrence of that linguistic sign, here and now. This form of expression of the linguistic sign, that is, the sign-design "Attention", on the other hand, occurs over and over again. We can read it on the road, in the train, at the airport and elsewhere. The expressions "Attention", "*Achtung*" and "*Attenzione*" in English, German and Italian differ in both usage and form, as do the sentences "Attention please", "*Achtung bitte*" and "*Attenzione per favore*". Nevertheless, we assume that the meaning is the same, at least in principle if not perhaps in every specific connotation. Therefore, meaning and expression, or the form of expression or sign-design, cannot be the same. Expression, or the form of expression, pertains to syntax, meaning to semantics.

- *Syntax* comes from the Greek verb *syntáttō*, "I assemble" or "I arrange". In grammar textbooks at school, we learn that syntax means the theory of sentences. In the philosophy of language, according to the terminology introduced by the American philosopher Charles William Morris, *syntactics* means the theory of "combinations of signs without regard for their specific significations or their relation to the behavior in which they occur".[11]

10 Heidegger, BaT, Chapter 2, § 7, Section A, p. 31. My translation.
11 Morris, Signs, Language, and Behavior, Chapter 8, Section 1, p. 219.

- *Semantics* comes from the Greek verb *semaínō*, "I give a sign" or "I mark". *Semantics* is the theory of what these expressions, or forms of expression, indicate, namely, meanings. Therefore, once again according to the terminology of C. W. Morris, semantics is the theory of the "meaning of signs in all modes of signifying".[12]
- *Pragmatics* comes from the Greek word *pragma*, "thing" or "action". It "deals with the origins, uses, and effects of signs within the behavior in which they occur".[13]

4. What Is the Meaning of an Expression?

How do we get from syntax to semantics? Syntactics alone cannot simply deliver semantics. It must be supplemented by something new that endows the syntactics – that is, the physical constructs – with the dimension of meaning. What is this new entity needed by syntactics to deliver semantics? While it is not as visible as the physical events and forms of events, it nevertheless exists because without it, the expressions, or forms of expressions, would have no meaning.
The obvious answer of how we get from syntactics to semantics is through ideas. Merely syntactical or physical events are transformed into linguistic events by ideas. Ideas are not physical, but psychological – or, more precisely, psychic – events. They are events in the soul or psyche. Expressions, therefore, obtain their meaning from psychic events. This thesis was already being defended by Aristotle, whose "affections in the soul" are here to be read as "ideas".

> Spoken words are the symbols of affections in the soul and written marks symbols of spoken sounds. And just as written marks are not the same for all men, neither are spoken sounds. But what these are primarily signs of, that is affections of the soul, are the same for all human beings; and what these affections are likenesses of, that is actual things, are also the same.[14]

Written words, then, are symbols of spoken words. But while writing and speech differ from one person to another, the underlying ideas are identi-

---

12 Morris, ibid.
13 Morris, ibid.
14 Aristotle, De int., Chapter 1, 16a3-8. Transl. Ackrill with modification.

cal, and so are the objects of those ideas. This relationship can be visualised by means of a triangle, which is known as the "semiotic triangle"[15]:

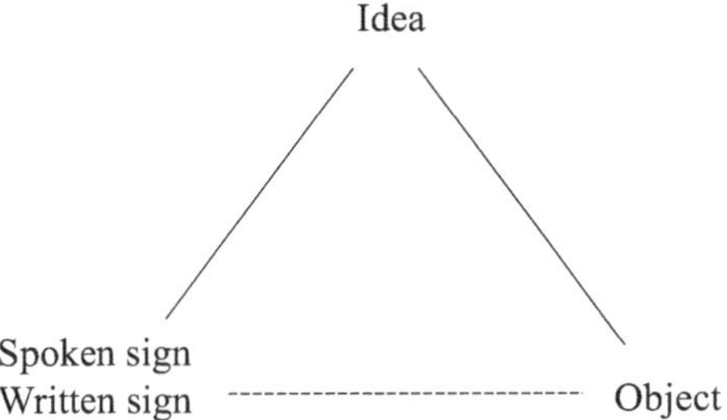

The written signs refer to the spoken signs, the spoken signs refer to the ideas and the ideas refer to the objects. The decisive element is that the words do not refer to the objects directly, but by way of the corresponding ideas of the objects: "Between the symbol and the referent there is no relevant relation other than the indirect one, which consists in its being used by someone to stand for a referent."[16] The word "house", for example, does not refer directly to the object known as a house, but only by way of the idea of a house.

Here an objection arises, which was first stated by Frege: "Ideas need an owner. Things of the outer world are on the contrary independent."[17] The owner of an idea is an individual who has an idea. How can ideas have different owners and yet be identical? I have my idea of a house and you have yours. I may be thinking of a large house and you of Anne Hathaway's cottage. But we cannot compare our own ideas with the ideas of others directly. We cannot slip into the consciousness of other people and check whether their ideas are the same as ours – despite however much a poet may wish to render his thoughts exactly as he thinks them. Thus, Heinrich von Kleist writes in his fictitious "Letter from one poet to another": "If I could delve into my breast, seize my thought and place it without any further ingredients into yours: then, to tell the truth, the whole inner demand of my soul would be fulfilled."

But let us suppose, for a moment, that we could slip into the consciousness of other people. What would the criterion then be that would enable us to

15 For the original version of the "semiotic triangle", see Ogden/Richards, Meaning of Meaning, Chapter 1, p. 11.
16 Cf. Ogden/Richards, ibid.
17 Frege, Gedanke, p. 351. Transl. Geach and Stoothoff, p. 334.

judge whether their various ideas of a house are the same as ours? In each case, the criterion could only be another idea, which would stand in need of a further criterion in order for me to be able to ascertain whether it is still the same once I have slipped into the consciousness of someone else, and so on to infinity.[18] Therefore, the meaning of an expression cannot be an idea. An idea is something subjective or private, but meaning is neither subjective nor private.

In order to counter the objection that ideas are subjective, Frege came up with the term "sense". He defines "sense" as the "mode of presentation" of an "object", "this word taken in the widest range".[19] Like the object, the sense does not differ from one person to another: It is not subjective, but objective. Therefore, words do not refer to objects directly by way of ideas, but by way of ideas *and* sense. This relationship can be illustrated by the semiotic triangle as follows:

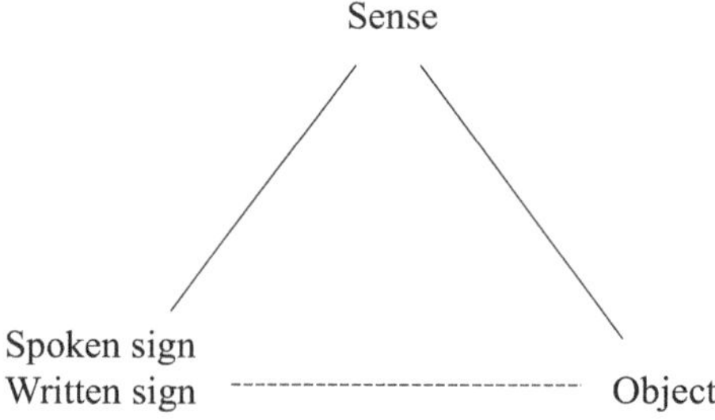

Here again we can ask the same question we already asked in relation to our ideas. After all, to say that ideas are the same for all of us is a postulate that has not been proven so far and probably cannot be proven at all (cf. p. 35). Likewise, it is only a postulate that the "sense", or "mode of presentation", of an object at any particular time is the same for all. It is legitimate and quite plausible to postulate that we all basically mean the same thing when we say "house". Otherwise, we would never be able to come to any agreement about the different objects called houses. But what is the criterion for the identity of the sense? It is supposed to be independent of the behaviour by means of which we demonstrate that we know what something is by doing something. When, for example, in response to the request, "Go into a house", we go into a house, we show that we know what a house is.

18 Cf. Frege, Thought, pp. 351-352. Transl. Geach and Stoothoff, p. 335.

19 Frege, Sinn and Bedeutung, p. 144. Transl. Black, pp. 152-153.

The construction of an identical sense, done in such ways, seems even more artificial than the positing of ideas as an explanation for verbal communication. This is why many philosophers find the notion of identical sense obscure.
According to Wittgenstein's *Philosophical Investigations*, it is neither the idea nor the sense that provides an expression with a meaning. Rather, the meaning of the word "meaning", in many of its occurrences, can be explained as follows:

> The meaning of a word is its use in the language.[20]

It is the use that turns the physical thing – the sequence of sound waves or the scribbles on paper – into a language sign. This relationship can again be represented in the semiotic triangle as follows:

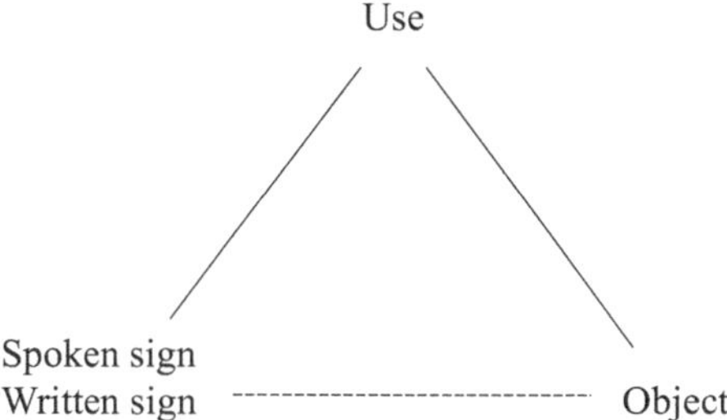

This means that it is neither the idea nor the sense that endows an expression with meaning, but that, ultimately, it is use that relates the expression to the object. Use takes its bearings from our conventions in using words.

5. *Meaning and Rule*

But when do we all follow the same conventions in using a word? This question of everyone following the same conventions in using a word concerns a special case of following a rule. When we use an expression to describe an object, we do so in accordance with a rule. When, for example, we use the expression "house", we follow the rule that bids us to use a physical form of expression – the spoken or written sign "house" – that corresponds to the object called a house. Speaking means performing ac-

20 Wittgenstein, PI, § 43. Transl. Anscombe.

tions – in this instance, speech acts – according to specific rules. Speech is action guided by rules. The philosophical expression "identity of meaning" is a way of saying that in any given instance, we are following the same rule, but what does following the same rule mean?

The immediate answer is that we are dealing with a state of consciousness. But this would take us back to the problem that we have already mentioned – which is that states of consciousness are subjective and do not yield the common element that would allow us to follow the same rule. Moreover, a state of consciousness – like a memory – may deceive me about whether or not I am following the same rule as another. On its own, it does not provide a criterion for deciding whether I really follow the same rule or only believe that I am following it. Wittgenstein puts it like this:

> And hence also "obeying a rule" is a practice. And to *think* one is obeying a rule is not to obey a rule. Hence it is not possible to obey a rule "privately": otherwise thinking one was obeying a rule would be the same thing as obeying it.[21]

A state of consciousness, then, does not guarantee that I am following the same rule. A state of consciousness is something within me, or an "inner process". But: "An 'inner process' stands in need of outward criteria."[22]

Another possible answer is that it is a disposition that makes us follow the same rule at any given time. A disposition is an inclination. If we were to go with this, however, two more objections would arise. We are instructed how to use words by the rules of usage. In other words, the rules of usage are rules for actions and they are normative. In the English language community, I am expected to use the word "house", and not some invented word, when I refer to a house. I can, of course, call a house anything I like, for example, "louse". However, if I want others to understand that my house is called "louse", but that I do not actually live in or with a "louse", I must bow to the rules of the language community and revert to the use of "house". An inclination explains why one does something, but not why one should do something, namely, act according to the norms of one's language community. Furthermore, I can apply the form of expression "house" to any number of houses. But an inclination at best explains why I am acting that way in a finite, limited number of cases, not why I act, and should act, that way in an unlimited, possibly indefinite, number of cases.

---

21 Wittgenstein, PI, § 202. Transl. Anscombe.
22 Wittgenstein, PI, § 580. Transl. Anscombe.

In the end, an inclination tells me as little as a state of consciousness does about why I should use the same form of expression to refer to the same things in a possibly infinite number of cases. An inclination, like a state of consciousness, does not entitle me to apply the same form of expression to any number of new things, as the American philosopher Saul Aaron Kripke explained following Wittgenstein.[23]

This leaves only the possibility that it is the conventions of a language community that cause me to use words according to certain rules. We follow the same rule when we succeed in understanding each other. Ultimately, this is trivial. Rather than solving the problem of how to account for the fact that we all follow the same rule, it only makes it disappear, as Wittgenstein maintains. Therefore, it is not a psychological meaning, or sense, that determines the rule, but the rule that determines the psychological meaning and sense. It is not until I internalise the rule that a meaning emerges as an idea; it is not until I project it into the outside world that a sense emerges as a "mode of presentation".

We are of course free to use expressions very differently, for instance, to call a house a "louse". I can, in fact, invent a private language that I alone understand. But I would have to define that private language, not only when I revert to a public language, but also for myself, saying, for example, that "louse", for me, means "house". With such a language, I would also prevent myself from communicating with other people. I could, when greeting someone, lower my hand, instead of raising it, or stand on my head, but I would probably be declared a madman: This is how the existing customs of a language community cause me to perform linguistic actions according to the rules of that community. We thus follow rules blindly, that is, without any justification by states of consciousness or inclinations. However, we are not wrong if we follow them as the result of social training. Our justification, or reason, for following the same rule, then, lies in the cause of that effect, that is, in the social training by a language community to which we have submitted since our childhood. We thus copy the words and sentences of our parents and teachers. Our words are the words of others. We speak the language of the language community in which we grew up. We may also say that it is the *institutions* of the usage of a language community that cause us to follow the same rule on each occasion: "A game, a language, a rule is an institution."[24]

---

23 This point is developed in particular in Kripke, Wittgenstein on Rules, Chapter 2, pp. 7-54.

24 Wittgenstein, Remarks on the Foundation of Mathematics, VI, p. 32.

These institutions are embedded in the community's forms of life; they can change, albeit slowly. The social forms of life, in turn, are embedded in the biological form of life of the human species, especially the genetic endowments which enable us to speak not only with phonemes, but with words and sentences. This biological form of life can also change, albeit much more slowly, perhaps over millennia, but "only in the flux of life do words have their meaning".[25]

If a particular philosophy can be characterised by the astonishing things it accepts as being its most fundamental ones, then from Wittgenstein's perspective, this would be the social facts of language usage.[26] They are the *Urphänomen* which I have to accept because I cannot resolve them into anything further. Thus, they resemble the "bed rock" by which "my spade is turned".[27] Here any doubt would become pointless, because such facts are the very conditions of doubt. Whoever voices a doubt as to whether we actually operate with language conventions has to operate with language conventions, that is, with meanings, too.

That is why such accidental empirical facts are in practice exempt from doubt. They are fundamental in so far as our knowledge – to the extent that we can express it in language – is built on such facts. If we were asked why we follow language conventions, we would be able to answer with Wittgenstein that that is just what we do: "We can only *describe* and say human life is like that."[28]

Yet, this is not the last word. In fact, Wittgenstein writes:

> For a large class of cases – though not for all – in which we employ the word "meaning" it can be defined thus: the meaning of a word is its use in the language.[29]

The fact is, however, that the use theory of meaning does not cover all cases of meaning. If use always determined meaning, then we would be

---

25 Wittgenstein, LS, § 913. Cf. my article, Lebensform oder Lebensformen, pp. 270-276.

26 See Bernays, 1959: "Perhaps the different philosophical standpoints can be characterised by the astonishing things they accept as ultimate ones. In Wittgenstein's philosophy, these are sociological facts." 5. Transl. Reck with small modifications.

27 Cf. Wittgenstein, PI § 217: "If I have exhausted the justifications I have reached bedrock, and my spade is turned. Then I am inclined to say: 'This is simply what I do'." Transl. Anscombe.

28 Wittgenstein, BFBG, p. 31; "describe" emphasised. Transl. Miles.

29 Wittgenstein, PI, § 43. Transl. Anscombe.

bound by the history of use. But, in new usages, the intention of the speaker cannot help but also play a significant role. This fact is key to a theory proposed by Paul Grice and emphasised by Donald Davidson. Thus, for Grice, "A meant something by x" is roughly equivalent to

> A uttered x with the intention of inducing a belief by means of the recognition of this intention.[30]

The paradigmatic example for Davidson are "malapropisms", that is, the use of an incorrect word in place of the correct word with a similar sound.[31] The expression goes back to Mrs Malaprop, a figure in Sheridan's play "The Rivals". Malapropisms often occur as errors in natural speech. Thus, Mrs Malaprop said: "[...] illiterate him, I say, quite from your memory"[32] when she meant "obliterate". This theory is also called the Humpty-Dumpty Theory of Meaning with reference to Lewis Carroll's *Alice's Adventures in Wonderland*: "When I use a word it means just what I choose it to mean."

An example is philosophical terminology itself. This terminology lives from the use of words in the ordinary language, but philosophers often give new meanings to these words. To take just one example: Philosopher (*philosophos*) originally meant someone who is acquainted with wisdom. For Plato, a philosopher is someone who strives for wisdom and to philosophise is the corresponding activity of striving for wisdom by giving and accepting arguments.[33] *Ousia* (lat. *substantia*) originally meant that which is one's own, or one's property. Plato gave a new meaning to this noun, that of essence.[34] Thus, use must be supplemented by intention. Modifying Wittgenstein, we could say, "only in the flux of use and intention do words have their meaning".

---

30 Grice, Meaning, p. 384.
31 Davidson, James Joyce, p. 143.
32 *The Rivals*, Act I, Scene II.
33 Cf. *Apology*, 28 c.
34 *Euthyphro*, 11 b.

III. Knowledge

1. Sensation and Argument

We acquire knowledge partly through sensory perception and partly through reflection. From time immemorial, sensation, and sight in particular, has been regarded as the prototype of knowledge acquisition. We acquire knowledge by keeping our eyes open and absorbing the world through them. If we were to close our eyes or lose our sight, we would acquire less knowledge.

But what kind of knowledge do we acquire through our eyes? Do we see "mere sense data" – red spots, for example – in our field of vision? No. We perceive "sense data" as something particular, as we do when we hear voices and read texts. If, for example, we see a red spot, it could be a wine stain on a tablecloth. If we hear a whistling in the mountains, it could be the whistling of a marmot. If we smell an odour, it could be the odour of a cigar. If we taste something sour, it could be the taste of lemon juice. If we touch a cold object in the dark, we might think it is a key. The following shape, ⌧, can, for example, be seen as an envelope, as a pitched roof (from above), or as a roof truss (from below).

Likewise, if we look at human beings, we, as a rule, perceive not merely bodies, but men, women, children, bank clerks, workers, asylum seekers or something like "the motley crew of humanity" (Wilhelm Busch). The French novelist Marcel Proust writes: "Even the simple act which we describe as 'seeing someone we know' is, to some extent, an intellectual process. We pack the physical outline of the creature we see with all the ideas we have already formed about him, and in the complete picture of him which we compose in our minds those ideas have certainly the principal place."[1]

What a person sees depends both on what he is looking at and on "what his previous visual-conceptual experience has taught him to see".[2] This visual-conceptual experience can be conceptualized yet again. The radiant look of a woman can be conceptualized as "beautiful like in a dream"

---

1 A la recherche du temps perdu, Volume 1, Du coté de chez Swann, Part 1, Combray. Transl. C. K. Scott-Moncrieff.

2 Kuhn, Structure, Chapter 10, p. 113.

(*traumschön*) and "anxious from longing" (*sehnsuchtsbang*), as in Franz Lehar's operetta *The Land of Smiles.*

Not only in everyday or poetic perception, but also in scientific perception, do we see a thing as a particular thing and not as a thing in general. As Thomas Kuhn (1922-1996) writes in *The Structure of Scientific Revolutions*: "When Aristotle and Galileo looked at swinging stones, the first saw constrained fall, the second a pendulum."[3] It is not possible to build a theory on the basis of pure observation, even in the empirical sciences. Observation always involves a theory. Observation and theory merge into one, so to speak. The more we know, the more we see a thing as a particular thing. The more species of flowers we come to know, the more we recognise the specificity of individual flowers. It is not until we analyse these sensory impressions that we can try to distinguish "pure" sense data from our interpretation of them. This is the case even though there may be no sharp dividing line between data and interpretation themselves. Sensation is mediated through the "lenses" of our interpretation. There is no such thing as unmediated sensory *knowledge*. Sensory knowledge that is unmediated, like a pure sense datum, is basically an abstraction.

In fact, sense perception is a relationship between (a) a perception *and* (b) a sense datum, that is perceived as (c) a particular thing. It is a tripartite relationship. The sense datum can be perceived from two different angles: on the one hand, in its physical or chemical aspect and, on the other, as a phenomenal fact.

A sense datum can thus be analysed physically or chemically. Lightning, for example, is a high-voltage electrical discharge of short duration. But, however we analyse this datum, it must affect our sense organs if it is to be accessible to us at all on the phenomenal level. The electrical discharge affects our retina. Our eye has a *causal* relationship with its surroundings and it is through this relationship that it experiences any changes taking place in the retina. According to the causal theory of perception, a causal relationship is *necessary*, if we are to have any knowledge at all that involves sensory experience.

Some changes in the world are forwarded to the nervous system and the brain as signals. Such a change generates a sensation and, in the present instance of lightning, a sensation of light. This is then interpreted as something specific, as the perception of a flash of lightning. The same principle applies to hearing, smelling, tasting and touching. One example might be when we interpret certain sound waves as the solitary song of a blackbird

---

3 Kuhn, ibid. p. 121.

before a thunderstorm. In addition to this more basic contribution made by consciousness, a more creative contribution is most clearly seen in connection with ambiguous things, such as the ⊠ shape mentioned above.

Sensory knowledge contains a passive and an active component. The passive component is made up of what the body absorbs, that is, a stimulus and what a stimulus generates – that which we call a perception. The active component is what we make of a perception. The decisive factor, according to the causal theory of perception, is that our sensory knowledge is necessarily limited from the outset. We are unable to perceive things that do not affect our senses or exchange any of their physical energy with our senses. For example, we can imagine a thunderstorm through "inner listening", and the music of Beethoven can make us hear one in the fourth movement of his Pastoral Symphony. Nevertheless, while listening to the Pastoral Symphony, we cannot see any lightning with our actual eyes because there is no physical lightning occurring.

On another note, beyond seeing or hearing them, we can foresee and predict future thunderstorms. Although sensory perception is the prototype of knowledge acquisition, it is not the only form of it. On its own, sensory perception would restrict us to the present and make us unable either to draw conclusions from the past or to arrive at inferences about the future.

Having said this, even if we were given sensory perception together with the memory of other sensory impressions we have received, we would still be unable to formulate one single scientific law. Moreover, there are forms of knowledge (mathematical and logical knowledge in particular) that cannot be acquired through sense perception alone. Thus, in addition to knowledge acquired through the senses (which depends on our interpretation of things) we must assume the existence of a further source of knowledge acquired not through sensory perception, but through what we call reflection.

Reflection is marked by making use of *reason*. By reason we mean *non-sensory knowledge*. This kind of knowledge is gained not through our senses, but through the meaning of words. Reason, in contrast to sense perception, draws conclusions. But it should be noted that our perception of a given thing as some particular thing is also based on conclusions we make about that thing. We see a thing as a particular thing because our past experience has taught us to see the thing as the thing that it is. Yet, sense perception does not draw any such conclusions on its own. Rather, it is reason itself that draws such conclusions. In addition to this fact, conclusions do not need to be expressly put into words but, when they are, this is done by means of what we call an argument.

An argument in the technical sense consists of sentences that have a certain relationship to one other. This relationship is inferential. The sentences that contain the reasons for an inference are called the premises; the sentence that contains the inference is called the conclusion. Hence, an argument consists of a premise, or a number of premises, and a conclusion. Two types of argument are particularly important: deductive arguments and inductive arguments.

2. *Deductive and Inductive Arguments*

Let us consider these two types of argument by way of two simple examples (the line between the premises and the conclusion represents the term "therefore"):

All humans are mortal.
All philosophers are human.
____
All philosophers are mortal.

This is an example of a deductive argument. The following features apply to deductive arguments:

(1) If all of the premises are true, and the inference drawn from the premises is done according to valid rules, it is necessary that the conclusion also be true. The conclusion of a valid deductive argument thus *preserves the truth* of its premises. In this example, the conclusion "All philosophers are mortal" preserves the truth of the premises "All humans are mortal" and "All philosophers are human".

Here, as with all arguments, we need to make a distinction between the truth of the premises on which the argument is built, and that of the conclusion and the validity of the argument itself. In speaking of the *truth* of an argument, we refer to *either* (a) the premises or (b) the conclusion of that argument. In speaking of the *validity* of an argument, we are speaking of *both* (a) the premises and (b) the conclusion of that argument.

A deductive argument is valid if the conclusion follows from the premises. The conclusion follows from the premises if the argument takes a form which makes it impossible that the premises are true and the conclusion is false. In a valid deductive argument, the affirmation of the premises and the affirmation of the conclusion therefore does not result in a logical contradiction between the premises and the conclusion.

A logical contradiction is the conjunction of a proposition with the negation of that proposition. For example, a logical contradiction arises when we assert that (a) all humans are mortal and (b) all philosophers are human, but not that (c) all philosophers are mortal. If all humans are mortal and all philosophers are human, then it is necessarily true that all philosophers are also mortal. To say that philosophers are both mortal and not mortal – combining the affirmation of the premises with the negation of the conclusion – would be a logical contradiction. Because the affirmation of the premises and the negation of the conclusion results in a contradiction, the argument above is valid.

Yet, the argument would also be valid if it came to light that not all humans are mortal and some are in fact immortal, or that not all philosophers are human and some are in fact non-human. For it would still be a logical contradiction to say that not all philosophers are mortal. In this way, we can see that the validity of a deductive argument rests only on the logical relationship between its premises and conclusion, and not on its truth. Therefore, the following deductive argument is also valid, even though it sets out from a premise that is not true and leads to a conclusion that is not true:

All humans are immortal.
All philosophers are human.
———————————————
All philosophers are immortal.

This argument is valid, although not sound. Only a deductive argument that is valid and has true premises is sound. A deductive argument is unsound if it is not valid or if one or more of its premises are false. We can therefore distinguish not only between *truth* and *validity* (cf. p. 45), but also between *truth*, *validity* and *soundness*.

Naturally, a valid and sound deductive argument need not have two premises. It can have only one. For example, the premise "It is not the case that some humans are not mortal" leads to the conclusion "All humans are mortal".

Only in a valid deductive argument is it necessary that the conclusion preserve the truth of the premises. This is not so in the conclusion of an invalid deductive argument. In the following example, the conclusion does not preserve the truth of the deductive argument, which only contains true premises, but which is nevertheless invalid:

If a philosopher owns all of the gold in the vaults of the Bank of England, he is rich.

No philosopher owns all of the gold in the vaults of the Bank of England.

No philosopher is rich.

Hence, a deductive argument can have true premises and still be invalid. A deductive argument is invalid if the affirmation of the premises and the negation of the conclusion do not result in a logical contradiction between the premises and the conclusion. In the example above, there is no logical contradiction if the premises are affirmed and the conclusion negated. The negation of "No philosopher is rich" is "It is not the case that no philosopher is rich". What follows from this is "Some philosophers are rich". There is no logical contradiction in asserting that although no philosopher owns all of the gold in the vaults of the Bank of England, some philosophers are nonetheless rich. These philosophers could be rich for other reasons. This is why the argument is invalid. A deductive argument, then, is either valid or invalid. There is no such thing as a half-valid deductive argument.

(2) The information content of the conclusion is already present, albeit in an undeveloped form, in the premises. The conclusion only *unfolds that knowledge*. Valid deductive arguments thus unfold existing knowledge. But this does not mean that our own knowledge is not expanded in the process. Thus, the conclusion of the argument

All humans are fallible.

All philosophers are fallible.

All philosophers are fallible.

contains an insight that some philosophers may not yet possess. We can also learn something new from deductive conclusions. There is scope for deductive discoveries. It is by no means the case that we have already drawn all of the possible conclusions from all the premises we know. Arthur Schopenhauer (1788-1860) cites the following example:

All diamonds are stones.

All diamonds are combustible.

Therefore some stones are combustible.[4]

This is a fact that we probably did not previously know, even though the new knowledge was already present, hidden in the old.
Examples of deductive conclusions are found not only in formal logic, but also in arithmetic and geometry. The best-known example of this is probably seen in Euclid's *Elements* (ca. 325 BC). In this work, propositions are proven on the basis of principles and claims. Euclid calls propositions "theorems", principles "axioms", and claims "postulates". Axioms and postulates are called "premises" by Euclid, and theorems are referred to as "conclusions". The method of proof consists in deducing theorems according to certain rules of inference. While Euclid does not put these rules into words, through this method, we stand to learn something we did not know before, or at least not in a fully developed form. Take, for example, the proposition "In any triangle the sum of any two angles is less than two right angles". This might represent a new insight for most schoolchildren.
Frege, too, argues that arithmetical truths are obtained deductively, but can nevertheless increase our knowledge. This fact, Frege adds, should "put an end to the widespread contempt for analytic judgments and to the legend of the sterility of pure logic".[5] Thus, the realisation that there are more prime numbers than he has ever been shown, or that "(a + b) × (a – b)" leads to "(a × a) – (b × b)", will increase a schoolboy's knowledge as much as the awareness that some stones are combustible. To take another example, our knowledge is expanded when we learn that there are some prime numbers with more than 258,716 digits, which used to be regarded as the largest prime number ever calculated.

Deductive conclusions must be distinguished from inductive ones. To show this, I will again choose a simple example:

All of the philosophers observed until day X have died.

All philosophers are mortal.

This is an example of an inductive argument, to which the following characteristics apply:
(1) If the premise or premises are true, it is not necessary for the conclusion also to be true, because there is no valid rule that allows the truth of the premise (or premises) to be transferred to the conclusion. The premise

4 Schopenhauer, W II, Book 1, Chapter 10, p. 118. Transl. Haldane and Kemp.
5 Foundations of Arithmetic, § 17, p. 24 of the English translation.

"All of the philosophers observed until day X have died" refers either to a day in the past or to today. The conclusion "All philosophers are mortal" includes all future philosophers. Yet, some future day could witness the birth of a philosopher who will not die. The conclusion here is fallible, because its truth does not follow from the truth of the premise. An inductive argument is thus not logically valid, since the affirmation of the premise(s) and the negation of the conclusion do not produce a logical contradiction between the premise(s) and the conclusion. The conclusion of an inductive argument *does not preserve the truth* of the premises, but merely *expands their content*.

Accordingly, the conclusion of a general inductive argument may turn out to be wrong if it is refuted or falsified by experience. In fact, no conclusion of a general inductive argument can be true in a strict sense, because no conclusion of a general inductive argument can be proven or verified completely. In order to verify a general inductive argument completely, we would need to be in a position to check all future examples, which are potentially infinite in number. In addition, we would need to include all future philosophers in our argument. In order to do that, not only would we have to be immortal ourselves, but, as I have said, one day a philosopher might be born who would never die. The conclusion above is confirmed, without exception and therefore indisputably, only up to the present moment.

Other conclusions reached inductively, such as philosophers being difficult to understand, are less well confirmed. In such a case as this, the degree of confirmation is not determined by the meaning of the words (although these must be defined with sufficient precision), but by experience itself. An inductive argument is never either valid or invalid, but always more or less valid and, even when an argument is *more or less* valid according to experience, it is not *more or less logically* valid, but *simply logically invalid*. A conclusion reached inductively can only be to a greater or lesser degree verified or confirmed.

(2) The information content of a conclusion is not found in its premises, as we see, albeit in an undeveloped form, in deductive arguments. Inductive conclusions do not disclose what we already know in a hidden form. Rather, they *project existing knowledge* into the future.

Examples of inductive arguments occur in most scientific disciplines. All of the natural laws go beyond merely describing the condition of the world to date. Even a simple case, such as Hooke's law, where it is stated that "The pulling force of an elastic spring is proportional to its extension", projects existing knowledge into the future. The fact that extension is proportional to pulling force is valid for all elastic springs, including those that will exist in times to come. Natural laws are not obtained by merely listing empirical data. Generally, though not always, they are articulated on the basis of a working hypothesis. They are, however, confirmed only by the empirical data available up to the present and are therefore fundamentally fallible. All of the natural laws that are valid today may no longer be valid tomorrow. Tomorrow the Earth may cease to rotate on its own axis and the sun may fail to rise.

Inductive arguments – I repeat once more, to avoid misunderstanding – are not logically valid. In inductive arguments, the affirmation of the premise(s) and the negation of the conclusion do not produce a logical contradiction.

Despite their logical invalidity, inductive arguments play a more important role in the empirical sciences and in everyday life than deductive arguments do. We use inductive arguments not only in many empirical sciences such as medicine, but also much more widely in our daily routine. This daily use of inductive arguments is shown in the following reflections:

Because the sun has always risen to this point, it will continue to rise in the future. Because fire has always burnt us to this point, it will continue to burn us in the future. Because bread has always nourished us to this point, it will continue to nourish us in the future. Because the chair we are sitting on has not to this point spontaneously floated up into the air, it will continue to obey the laws of gravity in the future, etc.

All of these conclusions are fallible, yet, without the instinctive subjective belief in their truth, we would not be able to perform the simplest, most mundane actions. That is why David Hume (1711-1776), in his *Enquiry Concerning Human Understanding*, described induction – or more precisely "custom" – as "the great guide of human life".[6] A belief in the "validity" of our inductive arguments is essential to our activities and survival in this world.

Conversely, in a world without laws, no predictions or plans would be possible and our expectations would be constantly disappointed. Such a world would resemble a nightmare in which we would be unable to take a single step in safety or eat a meal in peace. Conceivably, what was firm ground yesterday could dissolve under our feet today, the bread that had nourished us before could poison us now, and the chair we are sitting on could suddenly launch into the air. Even the most universal laws of nature, such

6 Hume, Enquiry, Section 5, Part I, p. 44.

as the principles of conservation, would become void. Our belief in the existence of natural laws would vanish. "There would be an end at once of all action, as well as of the chief part of speculation."[7] Nevertheless, the belief that the laws of yesterday and today will still be valid tomorrow is not, and cannot be, justified by a logically valid argument. Theoretically, tomorrow everything could change.

3. *How Do We Justify the Conclusion of an Inductive Argument?*

Let us assume that a creature capable of reason from a distant planet comes to our Earth for a day. It sees that the sun rises, senses that fire burns, feels that bread nourishes, etc. Does it therefore infer that the same will happen in future? Hardly. But if it has spent a week on Earth, it will expect these phenomena to repeat themselves, and, if the phenomena repeat themselves over a year, or indeed over several years, it will probably conclude that the same phenomena will repeat themselves forever. There is no logical justification for this conclusion. Nevertheless, we all draw it instinctively. A baby already learns from experience: "As soon as he cried he was fed" writes Wilhelm Busch.

Even animals harbour such inductive expectations, although they do not formulate them in a language, and it is doubtful that they are able to draw inductive conclusions at a pre-language level. Thus, a cat "expects" that the milk that nourished it in the past will also nourish it in the future. A chicken "expects" that the person who brought it food in the past will continue to feed it. However, as Bertrand Russell (1872-1970) remarks, it can end tragically for the chicken:

> The man who has fed the chicken every day throughout its life at last wrings its neck instead, showing that more refined views as to the uniformity of nature would have been useful to the chicken.[8]

On what extra-logical ground do we extend the content of the experiences we have had to experiences we have not yet had? By what extra-logical right do we project our past empirical knowledge into the future? This is the so-called *problem of induction*. Even though he does not use the term "induction", and he did not discover the problem, it was Hume who first recognised its full importance. Hume would say that custom is the princi-

7 Hume, ibid. p. 45.
8 Russell, Problems, Chapter 6, p. 98.

ple that enables the transition from what we know to what we do not yet know. In his view, custom plays the decisive part in both the evolution and the justification of these conclusions. Custom is why we make this transition, and why we are allowed to make it. This justification is also called the *principle of induction*.

Custom as a justification, however, is contradicted by the certainty with which we draw these inductive conclusions. We do not *know* that tomorrow the sun will rise, fire will burn, bread will nourish again, etc., but our certainty seems justified by the fact that such inductive conclusions – despite the tragic error of Russell's chicken – are rarely refuted by nature. The chicken has had its neck wrung. But this was because it had developed somewhat undifferentiated ideas about the uniformity *of nature* rather than about the uniformity of *human behaviour*. The sun does not set and rise everywhere daily, for example, at the North or the South Pole. But this does not disprove the fact that in our part of the world, so far, it has set and risen every day. If these conclusions could be justified merely by custom, the confidence based on the uniformity of nature would be incomprehensible. Why should nature follow our customs?

Hume's problem was presented in a new version by Nelson Goodman (1906-1998) in his *Fact, Fiction and Forecast*. While Hume was concerned with justifying our customary inductive inferences, Goodman shows that we need further reasons for our preference of accustomed generalisations over unaccustomed ones. Let us assume that all the emeralds we have seen up to a certain point in time (which we will call *t*) are green. And let us call an artificial colour, which is green up to a certain point in time (*t*), but red afterwards, "grue". Our experience up to *t* will support both inductive generalisations, that is, that all emeralds are green *and* that they are "grue". As both general hypotheses are equally well confirmed by our experience up to *t*, we can replace "green" with "grue" and, instead of "All emeralds are green", say "All emeralds are grue". In doing so, however, we are equally entitled to the conclusion that after *t*, all emeralds are green, and that after *t*, all emeralds are "grue". Given a certain quantity of data, and using such artificial predicates, we can find a large and indeed potentially infinite number of inductive generalisations on par with each other. For now, I will select only one.

Why do we not usually draw conclusions that project such artificial predicates into the future, for instance, that all emeralds are "grue"? Goodman's answer is that conclusions that do not use artificial predicates such as "grue" are better embedded in our usage than conclusions that do. That is why we choose one kind rather than the other, and we feel entitled to say that emeralds will continue to be green in future: "Thus the line between valid and invalid predictions (or inductions or projections) is drawn upon the basis of how the world is and has been described and anticipated in words."[9] But this answer is at least as unsatisfactory as Hume's. Why should nature obey our past and present use of words?

An apparent way out is to attribute probability to our inductive conclusions, if not truth. According to our empirical observations up to now, it is not true, but very probable, that the same thing will occur again. Here we have to make a distinction between the probability of events and the probability of hypotheses. In the first case, we attribute probability to *events*, and, in the second, to *hypotheses about events*. As hypotheses are formulated in propositions, we can also speak of propositional probability.

In the first case, the probability of events, probability is interpreted as the relative frequency of events in a sequence of events. This is empirical. Thus, it is an empirical fact that lung cancer occurs more frequently among smokers than among non-smokers.

In the second case, the probability of hypotheses, probability is understood as a relationship between propositions that partly imply one another. This approach is not empirical, but logical. Therefore, this kind of propositional probability is also called logical probability, although "logical" should rightly be placed between quotation marks. According to this interpretation involving "logical" probability, the proposition that all emeralds are green *partly* gives rise to the proposition that they will also be green in future. The proposition that fire has always been known to burn *partly* suggests that it will also burn in future. The proposition that bread nourished the hungry in the past *partly* suggests that it will also nourish them in future, etc. If the propositions about past observations are so well confirmed that the general propositions logically follow from them, then we have the extreme case of the probability **1** of the general proposition, that is, maximal certainty. If, however, the propositions about past observations are so badly confirmed that it is the negation of the general proposition that follows from them, we have the other extreme case of the probability **0** of the general proposition, that is, maximal uncertainty. Between these two extremes, we have a continuum of cases to which the "inductive logic" developed by Carnap applies.[10]

This "inductive logic" is very different from deductive logic, whose arguments are either valid or invalid. It is a logic of probability whose argu-

9 Fact, Fiction and Forecast, p. 116.
10 Carnap, Logical Foundations of Probability.

ments are more or less valid and whose conclusions are more or less probable. To quantify the "more" or the "less", the probabilities are allocated numbers between one and zero. Thus, it may be found that the probability of bread nourishing, based on past empirical observations, amounts to 0.999999. Therefore, the past propositions would imply a general hypothesis that "bread nourishes" to a degree of 0.999999.

To justify such a probability inference, however, we would need a legitimate reason for drawing conclusions concerning the future from past experiences. We would need an altered induction principle that would make conclusions concerning the future that are drawn from past experiences *probable*, albeit not *logically valid*. We can justify this inductive probability principle perhaps just because it has been true in the past. This would throw us back to the question of why it should also be true in future. To answer that, we would need a probability principle of a higher order making it probable that the probability principles to date will also be probable in future, and so on to infinity.

But let us assume that we can measure the probability of a general hypothesis without such a probability principle. In that case, we might prefer the well-confirmed general hypothesis H_1 to the badly confirmed hypothesis H_2 if the probability of H_1 is greater than that of H_2. The probability of H_1 is greater than that of H_2 if the past propositions imply hypothesis H_1 to a higher degree than H_2. Both H_1 and H_2 are general hypotheses. General hypotheses, like laws of nature, apply by definition to an infinite number of future cases. Therefore, an infinite number of cases to which H_1 and H_2 could apply are in the present unconfirmed. But since all the cases confirmed in the past amount only to a finite number, both H_1 and H_2 would have the same degree of probability – that being zero.

If we deduct a finite number of confirmed cases from an infinite number of unconfirmed ones, the difference between the finite numbers of confirmed cases will be the same, that is, zero. Infinity minus however small or however large a finite number still amounts to infinity. Thus, "*in an infinite universe* (it may be infinite with respect to the number of distinguishable things, or of spatio-temporal regions), *the probability of any (non-tautological) universal law will be zero*".[11] Yet, our universe may continue to exist for an infinitely long time, and what we have heretofore observed is only an infinitesimal part of the universe. This being the case, inductive logic

11 Popper, LSD, New Appendix, Section 7, p. 313. Italics in the original. Transl. Popper et al.

does not supply a good reason to characterise the well-confirmed general hypothesis H_1 as more probable than the badly confirmed H_2.

Nevertheless, we might subjectively regard hypothesis H_1 as more probable than H_2. We might underline this subjective probability by being prepared to bet on H_1 rather than on H_2. We are here, of course, only prepared to bet on single events, and not on any general hypotheses with an infinite number of unconfirmed cases. Only events can be dated; general hypotheses cannot. A "rational gambler" would take the objective chances into account in order to win his bet. However, faced with an infinity of unconfirmed events, nobody who makes a bet can win it. Thus, even in the case of rational gamblers prepared to bet, the interpretation of subjective probability fails to supply a logical reason for regarding the general hypothesis H_1 as more probable than H_2.[12]

It is for this reason that Karl Popper (1902-1994) in *The Logic of Scientific Discovery* chose a different route. He argues that empirical laws are neither completely verifiable nor probable. At the same time, they can be refuted, or falsified, by a single counter-example. For instance, the proposition "All ravens are black" can be refuted by the existence of a single white raven, unless we believe that blackness is an essential characteristic of a raven and therefore do not call a white raven a raven in the first place. Yet I once saw a white raven in the Negev Desert that was called a raven. If, then, empirical laws are neither completely verifiable nor probable, we may still adhere to them, so long as they are not falsified by a contradictory experience. Now, our usual empirical laws – for example, that the sun rises, fire burns and bread nourishes – are not falsified as a rule. Since they have not been falsified, they have thereby been corroborated. An empirical law or a system of empirical laws, that is, a theory, is deemed to have been corroborated if it has been proved true by experience. Since the empirical laws mentioned have stood the test of time, we can obey them.

What is most apparently undeniable about this reflection is that empirical laws are not completely verifiable, but can be falsified by a single counter-example, even if any counter-example is hypothetical. The above-mentioned white raven could have been an albino or fallen into a bag of flour or been painted white a short while earlier.[13] We must therefore make a distinction between falsifiability as a logical possibility and falsifiability as

---

12 For further information, see Popper, LSD, New Appendix, Section 9, Communication 3, pp. 359-373, Subsection 11, p. 368. Transl. Popper et al.

13 I owe this hypothesis to Feyerabend, Problems of Empiricism, Chapter 16, Section 14, p. 200.

an actual decision, and indicate precisely what would constitute a counter-instance of an empirical law. The empirical law "All ravens are black" is falsified by the existence of a white raven only if we actually define the bird in question as both a raven and white.

Popper, however, denies empirical laws any validity by his clear admission that Hume has posed a problem that cannot be solved by deductive logic. Popper himself did not find a positive solution to Hume's problem either, but he did isolate a part of the original problem and proposed a negative solution for it. Popper maintained that the conclusions of inductive arguments are not completely verifiable, but they can be falsified by a single counter-example. Having said this, though, Popper's negative answer still does not, by supplying a logical reason, solve the original problem posed in the question of what "our extra-logical justification for projecting our past knowledge into the future" is. There is no logical reason to project our past knowledge into the future just because it has been corroborated. Indeed, Hume's problem cannot be solved by logical deduction. Inductive conclusions do *per definitionem* not acquire any validity, as deductive conclusions do.

Popper's positive answer – that unfalsified conclusions have been corroborated – turns the original problem of what extra-logical justification we may have for projecting our past knowledge into the future into a test by time. Yet, why should any empirical laws that have been corroborated till now also be corroborated in the future? That is exactly what we do not know, and shall never know. Therefore, I believe that Hume, in spite of Popper's attempt, is right in principle when he says, "It is not reasoning which engages us to suppose the past resembling the future."[14]

4. The Induction Principle as a Hypothetical Postulate of Practical Reason

With the concept of corroboration, Popper brings a new perspective into play – cognitive valuation. If a law of nature has been corroborated, it is *worth* accepting. Hereby, however, he moves in principle from the area of theoretical reason to that of practical reason. Hume has theoretical reason in mind in the passage quoted above.[15]

---

14 Hume, Enquiry, Section 5, Part 2, p. 39.

15 Practical reason, in Hume's view, is only an imprecise and unphilosophical figure of speech for something that does not exist in reality. cf. Treatise, Book 2, Section 3, pp. 413-416. With this, he departs from both common and philosophical usage

Let us pursue this approach further. We want to accept Popper's critique and grant the laws of nature neither truth nor probability. We can, however, grant them a kind of extra-logical justification, that is, a justification not by theoretical but by practical reason.

To this point, we have considered only theoretical reason. There is, however, another form of reason called practical reason. This type of reason stems from the fact that we obviously draw not only theoretical but also practical conclusions. Theoretical reason infers what "will be" from "what was" or "what is". Practical reason, by contrast, infers what one ought to do. Those empirical laws that have been corroborated encapsulate the knowledge acquired by humanity to date. This knowledge has clearly proved to be an advantage in the struggle for survival. Conversely, it would be a great disadvantage not to know what we know from experience, even though not everyone would wish to put it in the words of Willard Van Orman Quine (1908-1992):

> Creatures inveterately wrong in their inductions have a pathetic but praiseworthy tendency to die before reproducing their kind.[16]

Let this survival value of the past experience of humankind be our starting point. From those past experiences that have been *corroborated*, we can deduce directions for our actions which should also be valid in the future. Because the past experience that fire burns has stood the test of time, it is expedient to assume that it will continue to do so, and that we would be well advised not to put our hands in the flames, insofar as this is to be avoided. Because bread nourished us in the past, it is expedient to assume that it will continue to nourish us in the future, and so on. Therefore, instead of understanding the induction principle as a principle that tells us what is, I understand it as a norm that tells us what to assume and what to do on the basis of assumptions that have been corroborated. The justification of this norm is not that I attribute any truth or probability to it, but that I see there is an advantage in following it. If, then, an inductive conclusion is not logically valid, it is as a rule advantageous. A ban on induction would amount to an invitation to suicide. It is, for example, expedient

---

introduced by Plato, Plt. 258 e: "Well, divide all cases of knowledge in this way, calling the one sort practical knowledge, the other purely theoretical" (Transl. Rowe).

16 Quine, Ontological Relativity, Chapter 5, Natural Kinds, p. 126. As I have remarked later, such a "pragmatic" justification of induction was introduced by Reichenbach, Probability, pp. 469-482, and Salmon, 1991, pp. 99-122. I reserve this justification for hypotheses that have been corroborated.

– indeed imperative – to assume that for some time to come fire will continue to burn, bread to nourish, and so on. If we were to assume that fire no longer burns or that bread no longer nourishes, we would burn ourselves or starve to death, as the case may be.

Of course, the survival value of our inductive generalisations need not be as obvious as all that. But if we were to assume, for example, that in the future ravens will be white and emeralds "grue", that stones will fly up into the air instead of falling down, that the planets will no longer orbit in ellipses, etc., we *would* be able to continue living but, sooner or later, we would find ourselves at a disadvantage in comparison to those who draw more "valid", that is, more expedient, conclusions. Since the empirical laws cohere among themselves, we cannot abandon any one or several of them without abandoning others. That is why it is usually the case that not just a single empirical law is corroborated, but a whole system of them. The pillars of the system are, again, certain basic laws, such as the principles of conservation. It is expedient to assume that such a system, which has been corroborated, will be preserved in the future even if not every single law is important for our survival.

To this extent, an inductive conclusion – embedded in such a system – is not logically valid, yet neither is it irrational. The alternative of assuming no inductive principle would surely be more irrational. Likewise, with our survival in mind, it would be more irrational to assume a principle whereby the opposite of our past experiences will occur. However, we are not dealing here with a valid conclusion of theoretical reason, but with a postulate of practical reason. This postulate is justified by the fact that, as a rule, it is expedient for our survival in a broad sense, even though it may not be so in exceptional cases.

An example of such an exceptional case is given by Popper when he recounts an episode of ergot poisoning in a French village.[17] In this case, the assumption that bread or corn is nourishing was not borne out. Such an experience does not, however, force us to doubt the validity of the general law that has otherwise been well corroborated. The ergot poisoning is an example of how a general hypothesis has been falsified as a logical possibility, but is nevertheless upheld because the counter-example is judged to fall short of being a counter-example for the falsification of the whole law. After all, it could transpire that the cause of the disaster was not the ergot, but the poisoned soil. Despite this odd and sad situation, it is more expedient to assume that bread nourishes than that it poisons.

17 Popper, Objective Knowledge, Chapter I, Section 6.

Inductive validity is, therefore, not a question of either/or, but of degree; this is due to the fact that there are also degrees of expediency. Thus, it will be more expedient in the near future to prefer an empirical law that has been well corroborated – for example, "The pulling force of an elastic spring is proportional to its extension" (Hooke) – to one that has been less well corroborated. These degrees of expediency could be quantified, in analogy with the degrees of inductive probability, as degrees of rational eligibility. If the past propositions have been so well corroborated that the corresponding law logically follows from them, we have an extreme case in which the degree of rational eligibility is **1**; that is, the degree of rational eligibility is maximal. If, on the other hand, the past propositions have been so poorly corroborated that what logically follows from them is the negation of a corresponding law, we have another extreme in which the degree of rational eligibility is **0**; that is, the degree of rational avoidability is maximal.

Between these two extremes, we would again have a continuum of cases subject to the logic of preference.[18] This is neither a deductive logic, whose arguments are either logically valid or invalid, nor an inductive logic, whose arguments are more or less (theoretically) valid and whose conclusions are quantifiably more or less probable. It would be a logic of preference, whose arguments are more or less (practically) valid and whose conclusions are more or less expedient in the sense of maximising expected utility to a greater or lesser extent. To quantify this expected utility, we could allocate to the degrees of rational eligibility numbers between zero and one, but only within a finite range. That way, we would be able to establish, for example, that, in a finite future, the degree of rational eligibility of the empirical law whereby bread nourishes will be equal to 0.999999, that is, nearly one.

Hence, while the induction principle is not a principle of theoretical reason, it is, in my view, a natural and legitimate postulate of practical reason. For conclusions that have been thoroughly corroborated or even shown to be completely consistent, it only makes explicit what we tacitly or implicitly expect, that is, that the future will be uniform with respect to the

---

18 For such logic, cf. Henrik von Wright, Logic of Preference, esp. § 1-8, pp. 7-20. It does not seem to have been applied to the problem of induction. Cf., e.g. Popper's disciple, Watkins, Science and Scepticism, Epilogue, pp.337-355. For the present state of the problem, cf. "The Problem of Induction", *The Stanford Encyclopedia of Philosophy* (Spring 2020 Edition), Edward N. Zalta (ed.), URL = <https://plato.stanford.edu/archives/spr2020/entries/induction-problem/>.

present. In this sense, the induction principle, too, is an *institution* that we tacitly accept.

An institution is a systematic framework of rules which normatively stabilises our actions, for the future, as it has done before. The induction principle, understood normatively, seems to be our justification for projecting our past knowledge into the future. It arises from an urge that is too strong to be suppressed without running the risk of endangering our own survival and that of the human species. In this sense, the institution of induction really plays the part of the "great guide of human life" (Hume). Like a guide, it tells us what to do. Like a guide, it gives human beings the following order: "If you want to survive and stay healthy, you should assume that, given laws that have been corroborated, the future is uniform with the past." Such an order is a conditional or *hypothetical* imperative. It remains one, even if the order is misleadingly clothed in the form of an absolute or *categorical* proposition describing the future.

It could, of course, also be asked why nature should obey our demand for uniformity. The answer would be precisely because this demand itself is "natural", in that it was always obeyed by the empirical laws of nature that have been corroborated. But, we might say, just because nature has obeyed this demand in the past, why should it continue do so in future? There is no theoretical answer to this question, and there will never be, first, because we cannot foresee the future of nature with any certainty and, second, because things can turn out differently from our expectations.

For this reason, Popper is right, in principle, when he says, "*We do not know: we can only guess*",[19] even though he is deviating from everyday usage, which sometimes allows us to talk of knowing when, in fact, we are merely guessing. Yet, it is equally right that assertions of knowing lay no claim whatsoever to theoretical infallibility. We need no theoretical infallibility here. John Stuart Mill (1806-1873) aptly stated this when he wrote: "There is no such thing as absolute certainty, but there is assurance sufficient for the purposes of human life. We may, and must, assume our opinion to be true for the guidance of our own conduct."[20]

Certainty and assurance are different things, even though this distinction is hardly ever made in everyday life. Certainty is something psychological, and assurance something practical. We do not know whether fire will still burn tomorrow, but we make sure that it will not burn *us* tomorrow. For the purposes of human life, we usually do not need more than this practi-

---

19 Popper, LSD, Chapter 85, p. 276. Transl. Popper et al.

20 Mill, Liberty, Chapter 2, p. 81.

cal assurance based on a rational – that is, expedient – choice. This practical assurance is probably the foundation of our certainty, of our belief, that our past inductive conclusions will continue to be valid in future. From a theoretical point of view, however, all inductive conclusions retain an irreducible remnant of irrationality. Theoretically, tomorrow everything could be different. Yet, it is a dictate of practical reason to assume that this will not be the case. In this refined sense, "custom" as *institutionalised* practical reason, is indeed "the great guide of human life".[21]

5. When Are Axioms True?

But even valid deductive arguments need not always lead to true conclusions (cf. p. 47). A conclusion is necessarily true only if all of the premises of a particular deductive argument are true and the argument is valid. So when are the premises of a deductive argument true? The premises of a deductive argument are considered true beyond doubt only if they are first premises. First premises are also called axioms. Their truth seems to be timeless and ubiquitous, "without, however, being provable by a chain of logical inferences" (Frege).[22] But what is the criterion of the truth of an axiom? A criterion is a necessary and sufficient condition of something. It is comparable to a litmus test.

Let us take the ninth axiom of Euclid's *Elements* as an example: "The whole is greater than the part." People think – as scientists and philosophers have done for 2,000 years – that it is its *evidence* that makes this proposition true. The word "evident", derived from Latin, literally means "plain to see". Whatever "catches the eye", in the sense of what is clear and obvious, is evident. Just as little as I doubt that it is bright outside when the sun is shining in a cloudless sky, so little do I doubt as well that the whole is greater than the part. Both notions make immediate sense; one to my eyes, the other to my reason. Trying to prove something that is evident (slightly modifying a saying attributed to Aristotle) is like trying to prove with a candle that something is bright when the sun is shining on it.

The axioms in Euclid's *Elements*, as he formulates them, refer only to finite figures. But what about infinite figures? In infinite figures, is the whole still greater than the part? If the part has an infinite number of elements, how can the whole be even greater than the part? In fact, if we follow the

21 Hume, Enquiry, Section 5, Part I, p. 44.

22 Frege, Foundations of Geometry, p. 262. Transl. Kluge, p. 273.

definition of infinite sets provided by Georg Cantor (1845-1918) in his *Contributions to the Founding of the Theory of Transfinite Numbers,* we find that the axiom in question is valid in one sense and invalid in another: "Every transfinite set T", says Cantor, "has subsets T_1 which are equivalent to it."[23] A transfinite set is an infinite set. Cantor's definition, then, simultaneously asserts both that the whole of the set is greater than its parts and that it is not. A glance at the following illustration will explain the apparent contradiction. Remember that the line is supposed to consist of an infinite number of points:

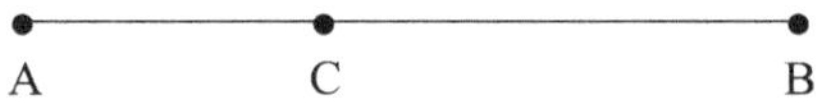

Thus, on the one hand, the whole of the line from A to B is longer than the segment from A to C. On the other hand, the number of points on the partial line AC is equal to that on the whole line AB, since both are infinite. Therefore, in Cantor's terminology, the whole and the part are "equipollent", or to use a more familiar term, "equivalent". However, it may not be immediately obvious how a partial set of points can be equal in extent to the complete set. I must therefore establish that fact by means of a definition.

The definition of parallelism was also assumed to supply a true proposition, which was called the parallel axiom. Euclid defines "parallel" as follows: "Parallel straight lines are straight lines which, being in the same plane and being produced indefinitely in both directions, do not meet one another in either direction."[24] This definition was used by others to formulate the parallel axiom, which is not found in an explicit form among the nine axioms of Euclid.[25] According to the parallel axiom, for every plane in which there is a straight line G and a point P that does not lie on G, there is a straight line G' that intersects the point P and that is parallel to the straight line G.

---

23 Cantor, Contributions, Part III, Chapter 9, § 6, p. 295. Transl. Jourdain. Part III missing.

24 Elements, Book 1, Definition 23. Transl. Joyce.

25 Instead, Euclid uses the 5th postulate to prove the axiom that we know today as a parallel axiom: "If a straight line falling on two straight lines makes the interior angles on the same side less than two right angles, the two straight lines, if produced indefinitely, meet on that side on which are the angles less than the two right angles" (Elements, Book 1, Postulate 5, Transl. Joyce).

This seemed so plausible that, to my knowledge, nobody seriously doubted its truth before the 19th century. The argument was about whether it was a first geometrical premise (that is, a geometrical axiom) or only a conclusion (that is, a theorem). There were many attempts to prove the parallel axiom, that is, to derive it from the other axioms in Euclid's system of axioms. Yet, these attempts were all circular and therefore faulty. A proof is circular if the truth of the conclusion is already assumed in the truth of the premises.

In 1816, however, the mathematician Carl Friedrich Gauss (1777-1855) proved that the parallel axiom could not be derived from the other axioms. This raised the question of whether it was possible to do without it. Gauss answered this question in the affirmative, and he constructed a consistent geometry without a parallel axiom, which, however, he did not dare to publish. Later, János Bolyai (1802-1860) and Nikolai Ivanovich Lobachevsky (1792-1856) also proved that the parallel axiom cannot be derived from the other axioms. In doing so, both felt justified – independently of Gauss and of each other – in constructing geometries in which the parallel axiom was no longer included. Later still, Bernhard Riemann (1826-1866) constructed a geometry with more than one parallel intersecting a point P. In fact, it was found that there were infinitely many parallel lines.

In the geometry of Euclid, then, we have one straight line G' that intersects the point P and is parallel to the straight line G. In the geometries of Bolyai and Lobachevsky, we have no straight line G'. And, in the geometry of Riemann, we have more than one straight line G'. All of this is no longer immediately plausible or evident.[26] In other words, mere evidence can give a valuable hint about the truth of axioms such as the ninth axiom or the parallel axiom, but we cannot always rely on evidence alone where axioms are concerned. Evidence serves only at first glance as a criterion for the truth of axioms. A criterion at first glance is a prima facie criterion, and a prima facie criterion can be invalidated by more accurate analysis.

Thus, in his *Foundations of Geometry,* David Hilbert (1862-1943) actually went so far as to abandon evidence as a criterion of truth. Instead of the fundamental concepts of Euclid's geometry, such as a point, a straight line and a plane, he uses corresponding variables, "x", "y" and "z", which are not explained in terms of their content, but which can in principle be interpreted at will. Geometrical axioms thus no longer need be evident, but

---

26 For an intelligible presentation of these non-Euclidean geometries, see Bonola, Non-Euclidean Geometry, esp. pp. 57-85.

are conventions arbitrarily fixed between these variables. They are merely syntactical characters without any content. These conventions must, however, be consistent and independent from each other. From an inconsistent system of axioms, one would be able to derive anything one wished.
According to a law of logic – if (p and not p) then q – any conclusion q could just as well follow from a logical contradiction. The small letters p and q are propositional variables standing for any concrete proposition. For example, we could substitute: If the parallel axiom is true (p) and not true (not p), then Hilbert is an unhappy man (q). But Hilbert did not want to prove this proposition in *Foundations of Geometry.* Axioms that depend on each other would be derivable from each other and would no longer be axioms. Hilbert separates the logical and formal element from the concrete, declaring consistency to be the criterion of truth and (logical) existence. Thus, he writes to Frege:

> If the arbitrarily given axioms do not contradict one another with all their consequences, then they are true and the things defined by them exist. This for me is the criterion of truth and existence.[27]

Only subsequently, as a second step, does Hilbert assign semantic content to the basic terms and axioms, for example, the meaning of "point", "straight line" or "plane", or the meaning of the Euclidean axioms, albeit without the parallel axiom.
The dismissal of evidence as a criterion of truth has an important consequence. When it was still in use, it seemed possible to claim that an axiom was evident in the sense of being true "in itself". Now it is no longer possible to maintain that an axiom is true "in itself", but only that it is true within the language community that accepts that particular axiom. Likewise, a proposition is true only within the language of the system of axioms concerned. Thus, the universal validity of the truth of axioms is restricted to a particular language community such as the mathematicians who share these definitions and the semantics accompanying them.
Having said this, we can also go somewhat further. Axioms need not, in fact, be arbitrary constructs. As soon as we allocate semantic content to these syntactical signs, and it is accepted by a language community, the constructs in question come to represent the semantic rules of that language community. And, as soon as these rules have stabilised, they become the semantic *institutions* of the language community. Therefore, in my view, the criterion of the truth of axioms need be neither mere evidence

27 Frege, Letters, p. 411. Transl. Geach and Black.

nor a consistent definition; it can also be the social fact of their stabilised semantic acceptance.
Such a language community can be very small, as it is in the case of non-Euclidean geometries, for example. Amongst the latter, it comprises those mathematicians who construct and teach such geometries. It can also be larger, as it is, for example, in the case of Euclidean geometry. Here it consists of all those who accept Euclid's axioms, including the parallel axiom. It can be even larger still, as in the case of the first Euclidean axiom: "Things which equal the same thing also equal one another." This axiom is also called the axiom of the transitivity of equality: If a equals b, and c equals b, then a also equals c. It is a view shared by most people, except perhaps by lunatics and philosophers – and denied by the latter only when they are philosophising.
The same principle applies to the *metalogical* axioms of identity and of non-contradiction. The axiom of identity can be expressed thus: Everything is what it is. According to this axiom, "no entity" is "without identity".[28] The axiom of non-contradiction can be stated as follows: No thing is, at the same time and in the same respect, another thing. We can combine both axioms and say, with Joseph Butler (1692-1752), that:

> Every thing is what it is, and not [at the same time and in the same respect] another thing.[29]

This is the ontological formulation of the axioms of identity and non-contradiction. The ontological formulation of the latter axiom goes back to Aristotle, who tells us:

> ... the same attribute cannot at the same time belong and not belong to the same subject in the same respect,... .[30]

In the ontological formulation, it is necessary to add the temporal qualification "at the same time".
In the logic of the modern age, these axioms have also been called laws of thought and formulated without temporal qualifications. The axiom of identity has been expressed as follows: "A equals A." The axiom of non-contradiction has been stated as follows: "A does not equal non-A." If for "equals" we use the sign "=" and for "does not equal" the sign "≠", they

28 Quine, Ontological Relativity, Chapter 1, p. 23.
29 Butler, Sermons, Preface, § 33, p. 25.
30 Aristotle, Metaphysics, Book 4, Chapter 4, 1005b19-20. Transl. Ross.

will read "A = A" and "A ≠ non-A". This is the psychological formulation of the axioms of identity and non-contradiction.

But modern logic in its mathematical form, as founded by Frege, no longer talks about laws of thought. It wanted to shed the subjective element and the "unhealthy psychological fast" or psychological burden attached to our opinions, ideas, judgments and inferences, and thereby penetrate to objective truth. Moreover, these axioms do not so much *de*scribe *how* we really think, but rather *pre*scribe how we *ought* to think. We can, of course, also think illogically.

Logic is not, however, the science of the most general laws taken to be true but rather, according to an apt definition formulated by Frege, "the science of the most general laws of being true".[31] From "the laws of being true there follow the laws about asserting, thinking, judging, inferring".[32] That is why logic can also be defined as the general science of inference.

Objectively, the propositions or sentences in which we express our thinking can be perceived by anyone. The two *metalogical* axioms are now regarded as propositions. They can be formulated in various ways, the metalogical axiom of identity, for example, as "p is identical to p", and the metalogical axiom of non-contradiction as "not valid: p and not p".

If we were to substitute a concrete proposition for the propositional variable p, we would obtain, each time, the same truth value for these laws, that being the value of true. This is why these laws are also called tautologies. Tautologies (from Greek *tautologeín*: to repeat what was said) say the same thing twice. In propositional logic, therefore, tautologies are forms of sentences in which every substitution of a concrete sentence for a propositional variable will result in the same truth value, that is, the truth.

Let us, for example, substitute the concrete proposition "It's raining" for the propositional variable p. The metalogical axiom of identity will then be "'It's raining' is identical to 'It's raining'". The identity of the two propositions here means that both are either true or false. It does not mean that the first proposition is true and the second false, or that the second is true and the first false. Both propositions have the same, that is, an identical, truth value. This is why we also talk about the equivalence of the two propositions, and can say "'It's raining' is equivalent to 'It's raining'". If we choose to render the phrase "is equivalent to" by the sign for equivalence "≡" – three parallel lines, in contrast to the two lines meaning equality – it

31 Frege, Logic, p. 139. Transl. Long and White, Beaney, p. 228, with modification.

32 Frege, Thought, p. 342. Transl. Geach and Stoothoff, Beaney, p. 325, with minor modifications.

will read "'It's raining' ≡ 'It's raining'" or, more generally, "p ≡ p". This equivalence can also be expressed in terms of a reciprocal conditional relationship: If the first proposition is true, the second will also be true. If the first proposition is false, the second will also be false.

In the case of the metalogical axiom of non-contradiction, the following substitution occurs: "Not valid: 'It's raining' and 'It's not raining'". The propositions "It's raining" and "It's not raining" cannot be both true and false (at the same time and in the same place). Rather than reciprocally determining each other, they reciprocally exclude each other. If "It's raining" is true, then "It's not raining" is false. If "It's not raining" is false, then "It's raining" is true. But the law of non-contradiction is always true, if we add the necessary conditions, for example, that it refers to events occurring at the same place and at the same time.

We may call these axioms "metalogical truths" because they are present as presuppositions not only in Euclid's geometrical axioms, but in the axioms of any special system of logic.[33] For example, the two metalogical axioms mentioned above are presupposed in the first axiom of *Principia Mathematica* (1910-1913), the logical system created by Alfred North Whitehead (1861-1947) and Bertrand Russell (1872-1970): "1.1 Anything implied by a true elementary proposition is true."[34]

This axiom means that true premises result in true conclusions. Let us take the following conditional propositions as an example: "If it rains, the road gets wet." Let us further assume that "it rains" is an elementary proposition. Then this principle means that if the premise "it rains" is true, then so is the conclusion "the road gets wet". Likewise, the validity of a deductive argument presupposes that the affirmation of the premises and the negation of the conclusion result in a logical contradiction, while the affirmation of the premises and the affirmation of the conclusion does not.

Of course, a radical sceptic could also deny the metalogical axioms of identity and non-contradiction. Even though there has hardly ever been such a sceptic, his position could be very well formulated as a hypothesis. In order to negate the metalogical axioms, he would first be compelled to affirm them. If he said, "The axiom of identity is not true", he would be presupposing the following proposition: "'The axiom of identity is not true' is identical to 'the axiom of identity is not true'." But if he substituted the word "equivalent" for "identical", he would be assuming the proposition:

33 To my knowledge, the term "metalogical truths" for these axioms was introduced by Schopenhauer, Fourfold Root, § 33, p. 108.
34 Whitehead/Russell, PM, Part I, Section A, p. 94.

"'The axiom of identity is not true' is equivalent to the proposition 'the axiom of identity is not true'." Here "equivalent" is only a different word for "identical" that expresses the identity of the truth value. In both cases, the radical sceptic would still be presupposing the axiom of identity in order to negate it.

Now let us further imagine our radical sceptic as saying "The axiom of non-contradiction is not true". In that case, he would presuppose that the sentence "The axiom of non-contradiction is not true" and its negation, "The axiom of non-contradiction is true", are not true simultaneously. Yet by this presupposition, he will be affirming the axiom of non-contradiction. If he affirms the axiom of non-contradiction, he does not negate it. But if he does not negate it, even the radical sceptic can no longer advocate the negation of the law of non-contradiction. He cannot advocate negating it precisely because in order to advocate negating it, he has to affirm it.

If the radical sceptic could no longer advocate his own theoretical position, he would be constrained to withdraw from any verbal debate with his opponent and be condemned to silence. Since he would no longer advocate any theoretical position, he would indeed be irrefutable, albeit not because he was advocating an irrefutable theoretical position, but because he was no longer saying – or even able to say – anything definite, for any proposition he formulated would also mean its opposite. At best, he would be able to express his position in body language, for example, by shaking his head doubtfully if somebody stated the axiom of identity or non-contradiction. But even this doubtful shaking of the head would be unclear, since it could express either affirmation or negation.

In contrast, the metalogical axiom of the excluded middle or third – which claims with reference to any sentence p: "p or not p. There is no third" – is not true of every system of axioms in logic and mathematics. It is not true, for example, in the system of Luitzen Egbertus Jan Brouwer (1881-1966). According to Brouwer, mathematical propositions can be considered true or false only if they are provable or refutable by means of a construction. But, when dealing with infinity, we cannot assume that every mathematical sentence will be provable or refutable, with no third possibility between them.

For example, there are perfect numbers and imperfect numbers. A perfect number is a natural number that is equal to the sum of its divisors. Thus, the number 6 is perfect, since 6 = 1+2+3. The number 28 is perfect, since 28 = 1+2+4+7+14. So are 496 and six other even numbers, since their sum is also equal to the sum of their divisors. But to date, no odd number has been proved to be a perfect number. This does not mean that all odd numbers are imperfect. Rather, a sentence such as "All odd numbers are imperfect" is neither provable nor refutable by a construction, since there are infinitely many odd numbers. That is why, according to Brouwer, the metalogical law of the excluded third is not true of propositions about an infinity of numbers.

In my view then, axioms are true neither because they are always evident nor because they are laid out consistently, but rather because they are institutionalised in a language community. Those who fail to accept them do not belong to that language community. The institutions of a language community are not only laws of being true, *de*scribing what is the case in that community, but they are also rules *pre*scribing what should be taken for truth in that community. Thus, the institutionalist understanding of axioms shows not only why these axioms *are* true in a language community, but also why the members of the language community in question *ought* to follow these axioms.

This institutionalist view of axioms may seem sobering. Yet, if it is true, there can be no absolute justification of the truth of axioms, but only a relative justification in light of the semantic institutions of the language community concerned. Naturally, these must be consistent with and independent of each other. On the basis of this merely relative justification, we can, in my opinion, no longer assert that axioms are timeless and true everywhere.

IV. Truth

1. The Classic Definition of Truth

In the last chapter, I often used the terms "true" and "truth". But what is truth? This was the question asked by Pilate when Jesus said to him: "To this end I was born, and for this cause came I into the world, that I should bear witness unto the truth."[1] Jesus seems to know what truth is, since he takes himself to be the truth: "I am the way, the truth, and the life."[2] But Pilate, the unbelieving sceptic, retorts "What is truth?"[3] and does not even appear interested in an answer. A modern sceptic, Oswald Spengler, suggested the following answer:

> What is truth? For the masses, that which they continually read and hear. A poor devil may be sitting somewhere and collecting grounds on which to determine "the truth" – but what it obtains is just *his* truth. The other, the public truth of the moment, which alone matters in the material world of efficiency and success, is today a product of the press. What the press wants is "true". Its barons create, transform, switch truths. Three weeks of press work, and "the truth" is acknowledged by everybody. Its arguments are irrefutable as long as there is enough money to keep repeating them. Classical rhetoric, too, was designed for effect and not content [...] but it limited itself to the actual audience and the moment. The dynamics of the press demands *permanent* effects. It must exert *continuous* pressure on people's minds. Its arguments are refuted as soon as the greater financial power shifts to the counter-arguments which are presented even more intensively to all eyes and ears. At that moment the needle of public opinion swings round to the stronger pole. Everybody is immediately convinced of the new "truth", and considers himself awakened from an error.[4]

---

1 John XVIII, 37. Transl. King James Bible.
2 John XIV, 6. Transl. King James Bible.
3 John XVIII, 37. Transl. King James Bible.
4 Spengler, DW, Volume 2, Chapter 4, Section 3, pp. 1139-1140. Transl. Atkinson with minor modifications.

Truth, then, is "today a product of the press" or, as we might say, the media. Obviously, by "truth", Spengler means what is taken to be true. He is advancing a hypothesis about what is the case when "the masses" believe something to be true. The hypothesis may or may not be true, but we "poor devils" want to know something else – not what is the case when we regard an opinion as true, but what *the* truth, the objective truth, is.

Here we must make a distinction. When we say that someone is a true friend, we do not mean the same thing as when we say that a sentence is true. In the first case, we mean that the person concerned is a genuine friend, whereas in the second case – if we, for example, assume that someone's testimony in a court of law is true – we mean something different, namely, that it corresponds to reality. In the first case, then, truth is a property of a person or a thing; in the second, it is a relationship between a sentence and reality. The first kind of truth is also called ontological truth, the second propositional truth.

To put things more accurately, in the second case, it is not the sentence as such that is true, but the content of the sentence. If the sentence were true only as a sequence of sounds, a translation of it into another language, even with the same content, would no longer be true. Since the sequence of sounds is different in different languages, the sentence as a physical form of expression cannot itself be true. What is true is the content of that form of expression. This content is also called a *proposition*.

As a variable for propositions, let us use capital letters, for example, "P", "Q", "R", etc., and for sentences, lower-case ones, for example, "p", "q", "r", etc. In what follows, I will restrict myself to the second type of truth, that is, propositional truth, and not ontological truth. Since I have already spoken about the truth of mathematical and logical axioms, I will now concentrate on the truth of propositions bearing on the external world.

A proposition is true if it corresponds to the facts. It is false if it does not correspond to them. The proposition "Snow is white" is true if snow is white, and false if snow is not white. This conception of truth is based on correspondence and non-correspondence. Therefore, it is also called the correspondence theory of truth. It is a new formulation of the classic thesis that truth is the correspondence between knowledge and reality.

Aristotle, without using the Greek word for correspondence, put it as follows:

> To say of what is that it is not, or of what is not that it is, is false, while to say of what is that it is, and of what is not that it is not, is true.[5]

What is remarkable about this definition is that if we appeal to the correspondence theory in asserting the truth of a proposition, we do not even have to say that the proposition is true. By formulating a proposition, we are already saying that it is true. If, for example, we assert that "snow is white", we mean that it is true that snow is white. Conversely, if we assert that "snow is not white", we mean that it is true that snow is not white. Thus, if we say "P is true" or "P is not true", we are saying no more than we would in saying P alone. The claim of propositions to truth is so obvious that we do not even mention the word "truth" itself.

This is why, unless we want to stress specifically that a proposition is true, we can omit the word "true". In such a case, though, the word "true" no longer has a descriptive function, but rather an emphatic or expressive one. For descriptive purposes, the use of the word "true" in connection with propositions about the external world appears to be superfluous or redundant. For this reason, one can also speak of the redundancy theory of truth.[6] The redundancy theory supplies neither a definition nor a criterion of truth, but rather demonstrates the obviousness of the claim to truth in terms of the correspondence theory. The redundancy theory of truth is not, therefore, an alternative to the correspondence theory. Rather, it is an indication of the obvious nature of the claim to truth of propositions about the external world in terms of the correspondence theory.

2. *Objections to the Classic Definition and Tarski's Reformulation*

There are several objections to the definition of truth as the correspondence of proposition and fact:

---

5 Metaph., Book 4, Part 7, 1011b26-28. Transl. Ross. The Greek word would be "*homoiôs*", cf. Aristotle, De int., Chapter 9, 19a33: "[...] propositions are true corresponding to how (*homoiôs*) the actual things are, [...]." Transl. Ackrill with modification.

6 This theory was first advocated by Frege: "Therefore it is really by using the form of an assertoric sentence that we assert truth, and to do this we do not need the word 'true'. Indeed we can say that even where we use the form of expression 'it is true that ...' the essential thing is really the assertoric form of the sentence" (Logic 140). Transl. Long and White, Beaney, p. 229. The theory became well known through Ramsey, Facts and Propositions.

a) The definition is circular. How do we know that it is true that truth consists in the correspondence between a proposition and a fact? We would need to know whether it really corresponds to a fact that the truth of a proposition consists in its correspondence with a fact. In order to be able to judge whether or not our definition corresponds to the truth, we would need to be able to compare our definition of truth with the truth.
b) The definition is not epistemologically neutral. It presupposes a naive epistemological realism which holds that an external world exists objectively and independently of human understanding, for example, that snow really is white and not merely perceived as white by us. But how do we know that a proposition corresponds to a fact "as it really is"? In order to decide whether or not the proposition corresponds to the fact, we would have to know the proposition and to know the fact independently of it. We would, as it were, have to assume "the God's eye point of view",[7] who is able to see the two as separate from each other.
c) But since we cannot adopt God's perspective, the definition of truth as correspondence turns into an endless series of returns to an endless array of facts, a *regressus ad indefinitum*. We want to decide whether the proposition P_1, "Snow is white", corresponds to the fact that snow is white. In order to do so, we must first fix the fact in question in a proposition P_2. Only then can we decide whether or not P_1 corresponds to P_2. But how do we know whether or not P_2 corresponds to the actual fact that snow is white? In order to determine this – that is, whether or not P_2 corresponds to the fact that snow is white – we must first fix the fact in question in yet another proposition P_3, etc. Therefore, we cannot decide whether or not the proposition corresponds to the fact by comparing the two, because we have no access to the fact apart from the proposition. We can, of course, see the whiteness of the snow with our physical eyes. But nobody has ever actually seen the fact that snow is white with their physical eyes. The fact that snow is white does not exist outside of the proposition in which it is stated. While the snow can be physically seen, a fact obviously cannot.

For these three reasons, we cannot endorse the classic theory, as it was formulated by Aristotle, which claims that truth consists in a correspondence with reality (cf. pp. 71-72).
While there is a method that allows us to retain the classic definition of truth, it only exists in languages whose structure has been precisely estab-

7 The term "the God's Eye Point of View" is found, with a critique of the correspondence theory, in Putnam, Reason, Truth and History, Chapter 3, pp. 73-74.

lished in advance. This method which would allow us to retain the classic definition of truth was put forward by Alfred Tarski (1901-1983) in his treatise *The Concept of Truth in Formalised Languages*. In this work, Tarski talks about *sentences* because he believes that the concept of proposition is not clear and unequivocal enough. While this move marks a difference from our earlier formulation of issues regarding truth (cf. p. 71), Tarski's choice of terminology need not prevent us from understanding the principle behind his suggested solution. Naturally, Tarski does not have in mind sentences in a merely physical sense, as something we hear or see, such as a sequence of sounds or printer's ink. Rather, he means *the sense of* sentences involving claims to truth. According to Tarski, such sentences can only be true or false in derivative terms, by which he means that only the *sense of a sentence* – the proposition – is true or false.

Tarski formulates the classic definition as follows: "(1) *A true sentence is one which says that the state of affairs is so and so, and that the state of affairs indeed is so and so.*"[8] He sees the general pattern of true sentences to be as follows: "(2) *x is a true sentence if, and only if, p.*"[9] Here "x" is a symbol of any individual name of a sentence and p of the sentence itself. The expression "It's snowing" may serve as a concrete example of such a "quotation name" x of a sentence. It symbolises the sentence that it is snowing. Therefore, according to (2), the following is the case: "(3) *'It's snowing' is a true sentence if, and only if, it is snowing.*"[10]

If, instead of the quotation name x, we use the variable "p", then a sentence "p" is true if, and only if, p. The truth of a sentence "p", therefore, consists in the elimination of the quotation marks or in "disquotation", as Quine has put it. The sentence "Snow is white", for example, is true if, and only if, snow is white. This equivalent relationship between "'p' is true" and p is also called the equivalence formula, and is represented as follows: "p" is true. ≡ .p.

> With the help of the notion "satisfaction", Tarski also gives a more formal definition of a true sentence: "x is a true sentence – *in symbols $x \in Tr$ – if and only if $x \in S$ and every infinite sequence of classes satisfies x*",[11]

---

8 Tarski, Concept of Truth, § 1, p. 268 of the German translation of the Polish original. English transl. Woodger, p. 155, quoted without footnote. Emphasis in the English original.
9 Tarski, ibid. p. 155. Transl. Woodger, p. 155. Emphasis in the original.
10 Tarski, ibid. p. 155. Transl. Woodger. Emphasis in the original.
11 Tarski, ibid. p. 195. Transl. Woodger. Emphasis in the original, quoted without footnote.

> where S is the class of all meaningful sentences. This definition of truth depends on the notion of satisfaction, namely, the "*satisfaction of a given sentential function by given objects*".[12] These objects are classes of individuals. Satisfaction is a relation which assigns individual objects *a* to free variables. So, "*for all a, a satisfies the sentential function x if and only if p*"[13] means that we have to substitute for *x* an individual name of the sentential function, for example, "snow is white", and for *p* this function where all of the free variables in it are replaced by *a*. Then – in the example given above – "*for all a, a satisfies the sentential function 'x is white' if and only if a is white*"[14] whereby snow, for example, is an *a* which satisfies the function "x is white".

At first sight, this formula seems to be both trivial and a mere reformulation of the classic definition of truth. This is in fact what Tarski intended. But one key point of this reformulation is that truth is no longer a relationship between sentence and reality, but a relationship between two different sentences – one in *object language*, the other in *metalanguage*. A sentence in object language talks about extralinguistic objects, whereas a sentence in metalanguage talks about *the sentence that talks about* these extralinguistic objects. An object can be any extralinguistic thing. Thus, the sentence in metalanguage is *the expression* "p", or "Snow is white". The sentence in object language is *p* or snow is white. Since this definition of truth is a semantic convention governing how to use the expression "true", Tarski also called this "*the semantic conception of truth*"[15] or simply the "CONVENTION T".[16] A convention sets constraints on an adequate definition of the meaning of an expression already in use.
The advantage of this definition of truth is that it is no longer tied to epistemological realism, but is epistemologically neutral, at least as Tarski intended it. He writes:

> Thus, we may accept the semantic conception of truth without giving up any epistemological attitude we may have had; we may remain naive realists, critical realists or idealists, empiricists or metaphysicians

12 Tarski, ibid. p. 189. Transl. Woodger. Emphasis in the original.
13 Tarski, ibid. p. 190. Transl. Woodger. Emphasis in the original.
14 Tarski, ibid. p. 190. Transl. Woodger.
15 Tarski, Semantic Conception of Truth, p. 345.
16 Tarski, Concept of Truth, § 3, pp. 187-188. Emphasis in the original.

— whatever we were before. The semantic conception is completely neutral toward all these issues.[17]

The "semantic conception" of truth says only what the term "true" means, and it only says this about sentences in languages whose formal structure has been precisely defined in advance. Thus, it must be precisely indicated whether the sentence belongs to object language or metalanguage. For Tarski, "true" refers to a concept in metalanguage, *where* it is not redundant.

Here it is important to note that "the semantic conception of truth" is *not* intended "to establish the conditions under which we are warranted in asserting any given sentence, and in particular any empirical sentence"[18]: "In fact, the semantic definition of truth implies nothing regarding the conditions under which a sentence like [...] *snow is white* can be asserted."[19] It therefore does not yield a criterion capable of determining the point at which we are entitled to maintain that a particular sentence like "*snow is white*" is true. This being the case, the disadvantage of the "semantic conception" is that it provides only a definition of the term "true" or "truth", but no criterion of truth.

In contrast to the semantic conception of truth, the classic definition of truth claims to offer *both* a definition and a condition or criterion of truth. It tells us both what truth is – namely, a correspondence with the facts – and also when we are entitled to assent to an empirical proposition – namely, when it corresponds to the facts. But the classic definition, as reformulated by Tarski, is acceptable only as a semantic definition of truth, and not as a criterion. Therefore, any theories of truth based only on Tarski's equivalence formula seem to me to be unsuitable for the everyday and classic concept of truth. According to these theories, "true" is only a semantic predicate, meaning no more than what is contained in the equivalence formula "'p' is true. ≡ .p". In contrast, Tarski recognised, correctly in my view, that the classic concept of truth means more than the equivalence formula. Therefore, any theories built on Tarski's equivalence formula alone are called minimal.[20] It is precisely because of the unsuitability of a definition of truth that does not provide a criterion of truth that we must look for other criteria. Let us therefore examine five other criteria of truth.

17 Tarski, Semantic Conception of Truth, p. 362. Emphasis in the original.
18 Ibid. p. 361.
19 Tarski, ibid. p. 361.
20 Such a minimal theory of truth is advocated, for example, by Horwich, Truth, cf. esp. Chapter 2, Section 4, pp. 25-26.

3. *Five Criteria of Truth*

1) A first criterion would seem to be coherence. An object-language proposition is true if it coheres with other object-language propositions. Coherence means, at a minimum, consistency, and consistency weakly interpreted means, at a minimum, an absence of contradiction. The object-language proposition that the sun revolves round the Earth is true if it is consistent with a system comprised of further propositions, such as we see in the Ptolemaic system. At the same time, the proposition that the Earth revolves round the sun is true if it is consistent with the Copernican system. The consistency of a proposition with a given system can be interpreted, in a stronger sense, as meaning that the proposition can be logically derived from that system. Thus, it follows from the Ptolemaic system that the sun revolves round the Earth, and from the Copernican system that the Earth revolves round the sun.

What is correct in the coherence theory of truth is the claim that the truth of individual propositions is not independent of the truth of other propositions. The truth is usually not restricted to one proposition, but rather belongs to *a system of* propositions. Here it is an inadmissible simplification to isolate a single proposition and attribute truth to it alone. The coherence theory tells us only whether a proposition is "true" or "false" within an accepted system. "The Earth revolves round the sun", for example, is false within the Ptolemaic system. This being said, it should be obvious that the coherence theory supplies no criterion when it comes to choosing between two coherent systems, for example, between the Ptolemaic and the Copernican. A proposition or a system of propositions may be "coherent", but is it true?

2) Earlier, in the context of axioms, I introduced *evidence* as a further criterion of truth. But the evidence theory of truth is by no means confined to axioms whose truth need no empirical validation. It is also the case that propositions about empirical data can also be regarded as true, because empirical data also provide evidence. For this reason, we must distinguish between the intellectual evidence of axioms and sensory evidence of empirical propositions.

But, as we found with regard to axioms, there are also borderline cases of sensory evidence, where evidence no longer suffices as a criterion of truth. In Euclidean geometry, we saw this in connection with the ninth axiom, "The whole is greater than the part", and the parallel axiom. But it also applies to moral axioms. The authors of the American Declaration of Independence (1776) write in the preamble:

> We hold these truths to be self-evident, that all men are created equal, that they are endowed by their Creator with certain unalienable Rights, that among these are Life, Liberty and the pursuit of Happiness.

It is by no means self-evident that all men are created equal. If it were, it would be difficult to explain why Aristotle failed to realise it. He was, after all, convinced by the Euclidean axioms that I have mentioned. Yet, in Aristotle's view, certain people are slaves by nature. He writes:

> For he who is by nature not his own but another's man, is by nature a slave, and he may be said to be another's man who, being a human being, is also a possession. And a possession may be defined as an instrument of action, separable from the possessor.[21]

Not every slave by law is a slave by nature. Someone is a slave by nature if he shares in reason only to the extent of recognising it in others without possessing it himself. Such a slave, according to Aristotle, may be kept almost like a domestic animal, since he has a similar function: Both slaves and domestic animals "with their bodies minister to the needs of life".[22] For Aristotle, then, slaves have the "inalienable right" to liberty just as little as domestic animals do. What was evident to the Founding Fathers of the United States was not evident to Aristotle. What the Founding Fathers called *self*-evident was, in fact, *acquired* evidence. Likewise, to us, it is on the whole evident that higher mammals may be kept as "slaves" to be domesticated, exploited, slaughtered and eaten. Perhaps this will not be evident to later generations, seeing that it is now no longer evident to a growing minority.

Sensory evidence – as seen in the fact that a leg seen through the bathwater looks broken, for example, or that the sun rises and sets – is not a valid criterion of truth. In reality, the leg is not broken and the sun neither sets nor rises. Some people regard it as evident that there is a conspiracy against them when something does not go as they wish, although this might not at all be the case.

The main objection to evidence as a criterion of truth is, therefore, that evidence itself can hardly supply a criterion for distinguishing between *genuine* evidence and the *subjective experience of* evidence. Being subject to the subjective nature of experience, this criterion does not support the claims

21 Pol. Book 1, Chapter 4, 1254a14-17. Transl. Jowett, rev. Barnes.

22 Ibid. Chapter 5, 1254b25-26. Transl. Jowett, rev. Barnes.

to objectivity made by its champions. While evidence can serve very well as a prima facie criterion, in most cases in which evidence really does go unchallenged, evidence is often only a sign that we agree about a proposition. A proposition or a system of propositions can be perfectly evident, but is it true?

3) Agreement between a group of people is the theme of the consensus theory of truth, a view advocated, for example, by Jürgen Habermas (born 1929).[23] According to this theory, an object-language proposition is true if it can secure the agreement of all participants in a discourse characterised by the exchange of arguments. This does not mean that an object-language proposition is true simply because it carries the agreement of all. Those who journey towards the truth journey alone, as the proverb has it. But nobody seeks to be left alone at the end of such a journey. Even the consensus theorists know that it is possible for a truth to be recognised only by a minority or by an individual. There can be a truth before it has received the agreement of all or most people. The tragedy of many creative individuals, from Socrates to Robert Mayer, who discovered the fundamental physical law of the conservation of energy, was that their insights were not accepted by their contemporaries. An assertion can be true in principle, even if only a single individual has recognised it. In the event of a miscarriage of justice, for example, a convicted defendant may be alone in being clearly aware of his own innocence.

The consensus theory of truth does not imply the possibility of agreement between everyone in all circumstances, but only in the circumstances of an "ideal speech situation". An "ideal speech situation" is one in which all possible participants in a discourse have an equal chance to carry out informative, argumentative, expressive and directive speech acts.[24] In concrete terms, this means that opinions are formed in a conversation of equals, in which (a) nobody can force anyone else to agree by means of either material or moral pressure; (b) all are prepared to be convinced by arguments rather than insisting on their own views, come what may, simply in order to be right and to save face; (c) the prestige of a person plays no part; and a great deal more. "The ideal speech situation", according to Habermas, is "neither an empirical phenomenon nor a mere construct but rather an unavoidable supposition reciprocally made in discourses".[25]

---

23 Habermas, Wahrheitstheorien, pp. 211-265.
24 For a continuing discussion, cf. ibid. Chapter 5, pp. 252-260.
25 Ibid. p. 258.

But, we may ask, when is it that we know that such a supposition has been realised? The mechanisms of power, domination and instinctive submission to authorities may operate so imperceptibly as to make it appear almost impossible to decide whether or not the process of agreement has unfolded in an "ideal speech situation". Rather, the consensus theory of truth seems to be an ideal that ought to guide discourse, but that does not supply a criterion for determining when a proposition is actually true. Habermas himself writes: "To the extent to which it suggests a concrete form of life, even the expression 'ideal speech situation' is misleading."[26] Nevertheless, the actual consensus provides us with a criterion as to when a proposition is recognised to be true. In this formulation, what is recognised or regarded as true *seems* to be true because it is reputable. Aristotle puts it as follows:

> Things are true and primary which are believed on the strength not of anything else but of themselves: for in regard to the first principles of science it is improper to ask any further for the why and wherefore of them; each of the first principles should command belief in and by itself. On the other hand, those opinions are reputable (*endoxa*) which are accepted by everyone or by the majority or by the experts – that is, by all, or by the majority, or by the most notable and reputable of them.[27]

What is believed to be true "by everyone or by the majority or by the experts", and among these "by all, or by the majority, or by the most notable and reputable", can claim to be reputable or plausible. But that is all that can be inferred from actual consensus. The "most notable and reputable" of the "experts", even if they agree, may be in error – not to mention the fact that the "experts" usually do not agree anyway.

The future consensus of the experts, even if it occurred in an "ideal speech situation", is neither predictable nor usable as a criterion of truth. The truth of a proposition, or of a system of propositions, may be such that, within an "ideal speech situation", all experts, or at least "the most notable and reputable", must be in agreement about it. Yet, is what follows from the agreement of experts necessarily the truth?

Consensus is only a consequence of a proposition, or a system of propositions being true, but not a criterion for it. A proposition, or a system of

26 Habermas, New Obscurity, p. 161. Transl. Weber Nicholsen.

27 Aristotle, Top. Book 1, Chapter 1, 100a30-b23. Transl. Pickard-Cambridge, rev. Barnes, with modifications.

propositions, may have obtained the actual consent of all in real circumstances, or the imagined consent in an "ideal speech situation", but is it true?

4) A further potential criterion is the pragmatic theory of truth. This theory was anticipated on several occasions, before it was explicitly formulated by William James (1842–1910). Goethe, for example, writes in his poem "Legacy": "Only what bears fruit is true." James puts the claim as follows, although he does not refer to propositions, but to ideas: "True ideas are those that we can assimilate, validate, corroborate and verify. False ideas are those that we cannot."[28] Truth, then, is not something static, but something dynamic. In essence, it is generated by the *process of verification*. The criterion guiding this process of verification or falsification is *utility*:

> True ideas would never have been singled out as such, would never have acquired a class-name, least of all a name suggesting value, unless they had been useful from the outset.[29]

The criterion of the pragmatic concept of truth, then, is utility in the broadest sense of the word. Let us assume – to take an apparently plausible example – that we have lost our way in a strange city. In response to our questions, we are told how to find the shortest route to our hotel. This information is true if we actually make it to the hotel by the shortest route as a result of following it. According to the pragmatic theory of truth, the belief in the existence of an external world and the existence of other people is true, because it is useful for our lives in the broadest sense. The same applies even to the existence of God: "On pragmatic principles, if the hypothesis of God works satisfactorily in the widest sense of the word, it is true."[30]

Here it becomes clear that there is something unsatisfactory about the pragmatic criterion of truth. A person who believes in the existence of God will not believe in the existence of God because that hypothesis works satisfactorily for him – that is, because it has a placebo effect. Perhaps it is only because of this belief in the existence of God that he finds it easier to bear his fate. Likewise, we do not believe in the existence of the external world and of other people because such a belief is beneficial for our lives. On the contrary, it is because we believe in the existence of the external world and of other people that we are able to improve our lives and those

28 James, Pragmatism, Lecture 5, p. 201. Emphasis in the original.
29 Ibid. p. 204.
30 Ibid. Lecture 8, p. 299.

of others, as well as to change the external world to our advantage. The pragmatic criterion of truth seems to confuse utility with truth. Truth can be useful, just as true information can be useful, but it is not necessary that all useful information is true, and it is not necessary that all harmful information is false. True information, such as a physician saying "You have cancer", for example, may do more harm than false information if it makes things worse for the patient. Likewise, false information, such as "You have the heart of a youth", may do an aging heart patient more good than harm, if it improves his subjective well-being. The hypothesis of God has proved useful for countless people by helping them to bear the blows of fate and to withstand deep suffering. But does that make it true?
Further, the substitution for truth of "what is satisfactory in the widest sense" leaves uncertain what is satisfactory "in the widest sense". The pragmatic criterion of truth is too vague. Even if a proposition, or a system of propositions, were precise enough to be "satisfactory in the widest sense", it would still leave open the question of whether what is "satisfactory in the widest sense" is also true.
5) Finally, there is Charles Sanders Peirce (1839-1914), who identified the criterion of truth as the goal or ideal limit we approach by constantly following the scientific method. Peirce tells us:

> The opinion which is fated to be ultimately agreed to by all who investigate, is what we mean by the truth, and the object represented in this opinion is the real. That is the way I would explain reality.[31]

This reference to the agreement of all researchers suggests that Peirce also uses consensus as the criterion of truth. Yet, his criterion of truth is neither an actual agreement nor agreement in an "ideal speech situation", but rather the ultimate agreement of all researchers, which lies in the future. Undoubtedly, truth has a unifying effect, since ultimately every reasonable person must agree with it. This is so, writes Peirce, because "truth has that compulsive nature which Pope well expressed: The eternal years of God are hers".[32] Yet, this unifying force does not necessarily produce truth. Apart from the fact that it is not certain what the scientific method actually is, this theory also does not tell us when a concrete proposition, or sys-

31 Peirce, Pragmatism and Pragmaticism, § 407. Quoted without footnote.
32 Letter to Lady Welby, Dec. 23, 1908. The saying "The eternal years of God are hers" goes back not to Alexander Pope (1788-1744), but to William Cullen Bryant (1794-1878): "Truth, crushed to earth, shall rise again; The eternal years of God are hers."

tem of propositions, is true. Since we do not know this final state, we do not know either whether a specific proposition is already true or, if it is not already true, how far removed it is from the final state. Moreover, scientific research can, in principle, continue indefinitely. But let us assume that the ultimate consensus has been reached. This still leaves the question open as to whether a proposition that is the object of ultimate consensus is or is not true. The ultimate consensus could in reality be the ultimate error and the final doom of all researchers. Logically, a proposition can be false even if it has obtained the consensus of all future researchers. The final agreement of all, like the agreement in an "ideal speech situation", may be only a consequence of, but not a criterion for, a proposition or system of propositions being true. A proposition, or system of propositions, may become the object of the final consensus of all, but is it true?

4. The Surplus of the Concept of Truth in Relation to the Five Criteria

The open question that can be asked about all five criteria shows that none of them suffices for us to say that an object-language proposition P is true.[33] A proposition, or system of propositions, may be coherent, evident, suitable for consensus, satisfactory, or enjoy the final agreement of all researchers. Nevertheless, we can still ask, "Is this proposition, or this system of propositions, true?" The concept of truth, then, is an end, which contains a surplus of meaning that is not exhausted by the five criteria. The concept of truth – to use an Aristotelian term – is "an additional end" (in Greek: *epigignomenon ti telos*) or – to use the corresponding Latin expression – supervenes (from *supervenire*: to come as something additional) on

33 The argument appears in Moore, PE, Chapter 1, § 13-14, in connection with the question "Is pleasure (or whatever it may be) ultimately good?" in order to show that the meaning of "good" cannot be identified with that of "pleasure", p. 16. Here, I have applied the argument to the criteria of truth. As I later remark, this application has been anticipated under the name "idealistic fallacy" by Putnam, Reference and Understanding, p. 108, quoted in Rorty, Mirror of Nature, p. 308. Putnam was anticipated by Moore, Refutation of Idealism, p. 450. The term "idealistic fallacy" goes back to Ralph Barton Perry (1876-1957) in his review of Moore, Refutation of Idealism, 1904. The conclusion of the argument also appears in Moore, PE, Chapter 4, § 80: "That 'to be true' *means* to be thought in a certain way is, therefore, certainly false."

the five criteria. It supervenes on these criteria, but cannot be reduced to these criteria.[34]

The term "supervene" helps us understand two things: first, that the concept of truth is superadded to the five criteria and depends on them to the extent that, without them, truth as such would remain unattainable for us. Thus, with Tarski's equivalence model alone – "'p' is true. ≡ .p" – we would be unable to grasp the meaning of the classic and everyday concept of truth. Second, the term "supervene" indicates that the concept of truth contains a surplus over the five criteria of truth. The concept of the supervenience of truth expresses both the dependence of the concept of truth on the five criteria and the surplus of the concept of truth in relation to the five criteria.

This surplus grants us an important insight: A proposition, or system of propositions, is not true for us if it is only true according to one of the five criteria. This is so because we can still ask the question ("but is it true?") that has remained open. A proposition, or system of propositions, is ultimately true for us only when it is true in itself. It is not, for example, true for us that we have hit the jackpot simply because this coheres with our other convictions, is evident or is useful for us, and has obtained the present or future consensus of our fellow humans. It is true for us only once the cheque has arrived.

Yet, although the five criteria do not suffice to indicate when "P" is true, they are not without value. They remain as prima facie criteria, that is, criteria that can be invalidated by other considerations. The cheque for the jackpot may not arrive even if its arrival is consistent with our other convictions. Conversely, a proposition can be true even if it is not consistent with a system of existing propositions, as was the case, for example, with the proposition formulated by the first person who said that the Earth is not flat, but round. A proposition can be true even if it is not evident, as is the case, for example, with the proposition that infinite sets have subsets equivalent to the whole set. It can also be true if it is not met with consensus in the discourse of experts, as happened, for example, to J. R. Mayer's

34 In a similar way to Aristotle's use of the corresponding term *epigignesthai*, cf. NE, Book 10, Chapter 4, 1174b33, here p. 147, I understand the term "supervene" in the literal sense, extending it to the concept "true", but with the difference that truth is an end which supervenes *necessarily* on the five criteria. In a more technical sense, the term was introduced among others by Richard Mervyn Hare (1919-2002) for moral properties that come over natural ones. For a precise definition, cf. Hare, The Language of Morals, Chapter 5, Section 2, pp. 82-83, Chapter 9, Section 3, pp. 153-155.

proposition that motion turns into warmth. It can be true even if it leaves our feelings in the widest sense unsatisfied, as expressed by the saying "sad but true". Finally, a proposition could be true, even if it were never to become the object of ultimate consensus among all researchers.

We could try to establish other criteria of truth, like beauty or elegance, for example. Thus, Nicolas Boileau writes: "*Rien n'est beau que le vrai: le vrai seul est aimable.*" However, the same open question could be put to all further criteria of truth: The proposition may satisfy this new criterion of beauty or elegance, for example, but is it true?

This inadequacy of all truth criteria has the important consequence that we are left with no satisfactory criterion for determining when an object-language proposition P is true. This situation was already known in principle in antiquity. Xenophanes, for instance, wrote:

> But as for certain truth, no man has known it,
> Nor will he know it; neither of the gods,
> Nor yet of all the things of which I speak.
> And even if by chance he were to utter
> The final truth, he would himself not know it;
> For all is but a woven web of guesses.[35]

The "final truth" can be understood to mean the objective truth. Yet, even if someone proclaimed the objective truth, he would not know it. Why not? Because he has no criterion for recognising that proposition P is objectively true. We need to continually distinguish between the subjective process of taking things to be true, on one hand, and objective truth, on the other. This being the case, any truth P formulated by us will rest upon what we take to be true. The sceptical philosopher Sextus Empiricus (c. 200-250) expressed this fact with the following image:

> Let us imagine that some people are looking for gold in a dark room full of treasures. It will happen that each will grasp one of the things lying in the room and think that he has got hold of the gold. But none of them will be persuaded that he has hit upon the gold even if he has in fact hit upon it. In the same way, the crowd of philosophers has come into the world, as if into a vast house, in search of truth. But it is

35 D/K, Fragment 34B. Transl. Popper, Conjectures and Refutations, Chapter 5, Section 7, p. 153.

> reasonable that the man who grasps the truth should doubt whether he has been successful.[36]

5. The Classic Definition as the Decisive Criterion and the Ideal

So, when exactly can we regard an object-language proposition P as true? When are we able to say that "Snow is white" is true? Having noted the fundamental inadequacy of the truth criteria that we discussed in detail, as well as that of certain others such as beauty, which we mentioned only in passing, it would not be sensible of me to look for yet another criterion. We seem to be left with little choice but to return to the classic definition of truth, that is, that truth is the correspondence of knowledge and reality, or of proposition and fact. In doing so, we must also bear in mind that the classic definition of truth is itself a criterion of truth (cf. p. 76). In my view, this criterion is the decisive perspective from which to judge any of the other five criteria of truth. A proposition, or a system of propositions, may be coherent, evident, suitable for consensus, satisfactory and enjoy the ultimate approval of all researchers but, if it does not correspond to reality, it is not true. The classic definition of truth, then, can explain the concept of truth in such a way that it loses as little of its meaning as possible and at the same time acquires a meaning that is not conferred upon it by the other criteria – namely, coherence, evidence, usefulness or consensus – all of which reduce the truth to something ultimately subjective. This is why Popper could justifiably refer to such theories as *subjective* theories of truth.[37] Yet, one could very well point out that if a proposition does not *correspond* to reality, the concept of truth would seem to have lost the *objectivity* that we attribute to it. The subjective theories of truth do not give to truth "the position which is its due".[38]

Earlier, we voiced three objections to the classic definition of truth. If we are to maintain that definition as the criterion of truth in spite of these objections, we must qualify it by means of the following points:

a) The circularity of the definition of truth is typical of all attempts at defining key philosophical concepts. We cannot define key philosophical concepts without presupposing them. In order to define truth as the correspondence of proposition and fact, we must have a preconception of truth

---

36 Cf. Sextus Empiricus, M, Book 7, Section 52. Transl. Barnes.

37 Cf. Popper, Conjectures and Refutations, Chapter 10, p. 225.

38 Frege, Thought, p. 342. My translation.

as correspondence. Yet, this need applies in principle to any definition of truth whatsoever and, since this is the case, we were able to ask the question whose answer remains open about each of the other criteria, this being that "if the proposition P fulfils one of these criteria, is it therefore true?" Further key concepts, such as that of being or the good, are subject to analogous conditions. Frege is right to suggest that it would be pointless to resort to a definition in order to "clarify what is meant by 'true'".[39] The same, he says, holds for all explanations in this form. He writes:

> A is true if and only if it has such-and-such properties or stands in such-and-such a relation to such-and-such a thing. In each case in hand it would always come back to the question whether it is true that A has such-and-such properties, or stands in such-and-such a relation to such-and-such a thing. Truth is obviously something so primitive and simple that it is not possible to reduce it to anything still simpler.[40]

Frege would therefore probably refuse to acknowledge Tarski's reformulation of the classic definition of truth as an explicit definition of truth. An explicit definition is one that allows the replacement of what is to be defined (the *definiendum*) with what does the defining (the *definiens*). In order to maintain the classic definition of truth, then, we must not understand it as an *explicit* but only as an *implicit* definition of truth. Such an implicit definition can also be called an *elucidation*.[41] An elucidation presupposes, explicitly or implicitly, that the concept that is being explained is already known.

b) The classic explanation of truth presupposes epistemological realism, that is, a belief that we can recognise reality as it is. It assumes that an external world objectively exists, that snow really does have a colour, for example, and does not merely appear to us that way because this is how we perceive it. One way we can avoid this epistemological realism is by reducing the classic explanation of truth to a hypothetical realism, that is, by not claiming that a proposition corresponds to a fact "as it really is", but only that a proposition corresponds to a fact "as it appears to us". If we follow that approach, we need not know the proposition and the fact as two sepa-

---

39 Frege, Logic, p. 139. Transl. Long and White, Beaney, p. 228.

40 Ibid. p. 140.

41 Cf. Frege, Logic in Mathematics, p. 224: "Definitions proper must be distinguished from *elucidations*. In the first stages of any discipline we cannot avoid the use of ordinary words . . . We have again to use ordinary words, and these may display defects similar to those that elucidations are intended to remove." Transl. Long and White, Beaney, p. 313.

rate entities in order to decide whether or not they correspond to each other. We need not assume the perspective of God. In this approach, we need to know the facts, and only to the extent that we have put them into words on the basis of our observations. The object-language proposition "Snow is white" can be compared with snow that is white to our eyes, if observed in the appropriate conditions. Whether snow is white, seen from the perspective of God, is a question that we have not answered and we need not answer. "The God's Eye Point of View", seen from ours, would be something like a "view from nowhere". In contrast, all we are able to observe is a "view from somewhere", that is, a human perspective. From a human perspective, truth is not a relationship between a proposition and a fact in itself, but rather a relationship between a proposition and a hypothetical fact.

Historically, the classic explanation of truth came into being within a framework of epistemological realism. Aristotle wrote: "It is not because we think that you are white, that you *are* white, but because you are white we who say this have the truth."[42] Still, this is only true within a framework of hypothetical realism. It is only a hypothesis that snow is white. Seen against the sun, it may be yellow. This restriction must be accepted. In addition, we can no longer say whether a proposition, or a system of propositions, is true in itself. This is another necessary restriction.

c) We can also avoid an indefinite regression of proposition upon proposition by fixing the reality of the fact that snow is white within a hypothetical realism. In order to decide whether a proposition P_1 corresponds to a fact, we must already have formulated that fact implicitly or explicitly by means of another proposition P_2. Only then can we assess whether or not P_1 corresponds to P_2. Here we no longer ask how we know whether or not P_2 corresponds to the fact itself, because we stop at P_2. This provisional stop at a proposition that only reflects a hypothetical fact is yet another restriction.

With the proposition "Snow is white", we have chosen a simple example, which allows us to study the problem of truth better than a complex one. Here the provisional stop at a proposition P_2 seems justified. Unless we have fallen victim to a collective trick of the senses, we may hypothetically assume that snow – observed in the appropriate circumstances – is white. But what about the truth we call the objective truth? Our striving for truth seems to remain unsatisfied until we have found the objective truth. This

---

42 Aristotle, Metaph., Book 9, Chapter 10, 1051b6-9. Transl. Ross, rev. Barnes. My emphasis.

would be a proposition, or a system of propositions, that corresponds to "reality in itself". So long as we do not have that, we should expect objections, whether from others or from ourselves. The concept of truth demands an objectivity that cannot be supplied by a merely hypothetical objectivity.

What is objective truth may be totally irrelevant when we ask whether or not snow is white. Anyway, we do not in general doubt that snow is white. Yet, in some cases, it is very important to render a fact objectively, such as in a court of law. Every judge has the duty to discover the objective truth, so far as possible. It is the judge's natural working hypothesis that a fact – a road accident, for example – occurred in a certain way even if it is no longer possible in retrospect to recognise or reconstruct exactly what happened. In such as case, even a simple task, such as the reconstruction of a road accident, can be difficult enough. Here, a provisional stop at a proposition P_2 may not be justified. P_2 may be based on a delusion and in need of revision in light of a further proposition P_3. But proposition P_3 may need revising in light of P_4, etc.

The situation becomes even more difficult in the case of scientific or scholarly theories, whether about nature or history. Here, a proposition P_2 may need revising by P_3, P_3 by P_4, etc. – or a system of propositions SP_2 by SP_3, SP_3 by SP_4, etc. – to infinity. There is no supreme court that would put an end to the search for the truth. Nevertheless, it is a natural demand of common sense that there should be a "reality in itself", even if it cannot be known. And common sense is something scientists and scholars also want to have.

Let me demonstrate this situation once again by means of a simpler example, that is, the translation of a literary text. A literary text is a system of sentences. A sentence can render the original more or less faithfully or approach it more or less closely. In principle, this process of approximation can go on indefinitely, leading to many translations of classical texts. At the same time, a translator assumes that a sentence cannot be translated in any which way that may occur to him or her. Likewise, the translator assumes that a text has a meaning that needs to be translated. This meaning can be vague or ambiguous. Nevertheless, the translator assumes the existence of an original meaning, even though every concrete translation is only a hypothesis.

The trouble with complex scientific theories, which may be far removed from sensory experience, is that they cannot be directly, but only indirectly, tested as mediated by the "original" experience. For example, a theory about nuclear structure at average temperatures can be checked only very indirectly by data observed in a "cloud chamber". Quine even goes so far as to say that theories can contradict each other and yet correspond to all kinds of sense data.[43] He calls this the underdetermination of a theory by experience. Here, it seems illusory to test the correspondence of these theories to even a merely hypothetical "reality". Since both theories correspond to this reality, the correspondence cannot be a criterion for preferring one theory to the other. Here, the search for *the* truth seems to be hopeless, and we will probably have to content ourselves with mere coherence, consensus, beauty or usefulness (in the widest sense of the word). In fact, all of these are prima facie criteria which are perfectly valid at first sight. Empirical scientists, for example, are often obliged to rely on a purely pragmatic criterion of truth. A scientific theory that has been corroborated can be perfectly appropriate and usable, even though we cannot know whether or not it is true.

Nevertheless, even when dealing with empirical theories at a remove from direct sensory experience, I believe we must abide by the classic explanation of truth as a criterion – even if it means that here and now we may disregard Quine's notion of underdetermination (for which it is difficult to find an example in normal scientific practice).[44] If a theory about empirical reality satisfies all of the other criteria, but does not correspond to empirical reality, it is not true. However, both the hypothetical realism mentioned before and the provisional nature of any proposition seem to make this natural demand impossible to fulfil. If we are to hold on to it, we must elevate the classic explanation of truth from the level of reality to the level of an ideal. In fact, the classic concept of truth includes a value judgment that I have so far neglected. Georg Wilhelm Friedrich Hegel (1770-1831), for example, uses this value judgment when he writes:

> To an unbiased man, truth will always remain a great word and make his heart beat faster.[45]

Truth, as correspondence to a reality in itself, is not only an ideal, but also, as the case may be, an unachievable ideal, like "the God's Eye Point of View". The best we can normally achieve is correspondence to a hypothetical reality. Yet, there is still a sense in which this ideal functions as a moral ideal, precisely because it requires that we disregard our own angle of vi-

---

43 Cf. Quine, Pursuit of Truth, Chapter 4, § 41, pp. 95-98.

44 Cf. Quine's examples, ibid.

45 Hegel, History of Philosophy, Introduction, A, Section 1, b, p. 33. Transl. Haldane.

sion and our own personal interest. The poet Ingeborg Bachmann expressed this idea as follows, modifying Plato's image of the cave: "You are imprisoned in the world, weighed down by heavy chains, but what is true drives cracks into the wall."

It is an ideal that could also be described as objectivity with the meaning of "impartiality". What impartiality is will easily be understood if we remember Spengler's "definition of truth" as merely a "product of the press". If this were so, the end of the Soviet party newspaper *Pravda* – meaning "truth" – would have been the end of truth itself. A historian researching the causes of the Arab spring has to be as committed to this ideal as a physicist investigating the structure of a nucleus at an average temperature, or indeed the safety of a nuclear plant, or as a medical scientist testing vaccines against COVID-19. Personal or party interests, often financial or prestige oriented in nature, may be a strong incentive to undertake research, but they are not the kind of interests that scholars and scientists should primarily pursue.

Naturally, we always see things from our own perspective. The perspective of truth corresponding to a reality in itself would only be available to God. Obviously, God's perspective cannot be attained by human beings. While the human striving for truth has been compared to a striving for the divine, there are times when we would be happy enough to come across a mere angel who told us the truth.

What we humans *can* do is to try to disregard all personal prejudices and vested interests in order to represent a fact as it is. The method for achieving this is to compare our own propositions with the hypothetical facts and, if necessary, allow the latter to refute the former. Likewise, we must expose our own perspectives to criticism and, if necessary, allow them to be refuted by the perspectives of others. This search may, in principle, go on forever. That is probably the meaning of the indefinite regression, whereby every proposition can be tested against a fact, that fact against a new fact, and so on. While what will finally be achieved will still be no more than a hypothesis, we must stop somewhere, if only for external reasons.

It is also important to note that such a hypothetical realism goes hand in hand with a "naive" or "in-itself" realism, if we understand this in-itself as an ideal itself. This notion is, however, key to what science and theory need; it is this very ideal that has to guide the hypothetical realism of empirical research and theoretical reason. While we can ever approach this ideal, we cannot reach it. By means of a normative reorientation, we are able to preserve the classic explanation of truth (with its surplus meaning) if not on a factual, then at least on a normative, level. The classic explanation of truth is more closely tied to the demand for knowledge rather than to actual knowledge itself and, since this demand cannot be abandoned, neither can the classic explanation itself.

What we take to be the truth can only approach the ideal of objective truth in different degrees. No hypothesis can actually reach the ideal. One hypothesis can, however, come closer to the ideal by avoiding the mistakes of another. We cannot arrive at a positive definition of how close P – that is, the proposition we take to be true – is to the truth. We cannot measure the distance remaining between P and the unreachable truth. But we can define it in negative terms, as the degree of its relative distance from error. The hypothesis that the Earth is a globe is closer to the truth than the hypothesis that it is a disc because it avoids the errors of the first hypothesis. But the hypothesis that our lonely planet is a globe, slightly flattened towards the poles – that is, a rotational ellipsoid – is closer to the truth than the hypothesis that it is simply a globe. This is so because it avoids the errors of the second hypothesis, etc. Therefore, as time goes by, we may still hope to get closer and closer to the truth. Truth, like the morning, dawns little by little.

V. Being

1. The Four Meanings of "is"

Having characterised truth as the correspondence of knowledge and reality, it is time to ask "What is real?" One answer would be "everything that *is*". But what does "is" mean? Just as it was impossible to provide an explicit definition of the term "truth", it is equally impossible to grasp the meaning of the term "is" by means of an explicit definition. In any definition like "the meaning of 'is' is this or that", we would still be using the meaning of the term "is", which is precisely what we are trying to define.

The verbal noun corresponding to "is" is "being". Yet, we are no more able to explicitly define the meaning of the verbal noun "being" than we are able to define the meaning of the finite verb "is". If we say "Being *is* this or that", we are once again using the term that is yet to be defined as part of our definition of it. Through the meaning of "is", we imply that we understand "being", which is actually what we are trying to understand. Faced with the task of explicitly defining being (in saying, for example, "Being is reality"), we could go on to further ask if reality, *per se,* is the same as being. We would be obliged to answer this question in the negative since whatever is not real, but only imagined, is something that also *is*. Like the concept of truth, being is a key concept of philosophy that cannot be explicitly defined. We are therefore able to define the concept of being implicitly, but not explicitly. Like the concept of truth, the concept of being can only be *elucidated.* In elucidating the concept of being, we can become conscious of what we already know about it in an undeveloped, that is, in an unclear and indistinct form.

Moreover, like the term "truth", the term "being" is *ambiguous.* When we say "Socrates is", the term "is" does not mean the same thing as when we say "Socrates is a human being". In the first case, "is" in the sentence about Socrates has the meaning "Socrates exists". In the second case, it connects "Socrates" and "human being". In the first case, the meaning of "is" is existential. In the second case, it is copulative. The copulative meaning can, in turn, be broken down further into three different meanings.

If we say "Socrates is a human being", we mean that Socrates is a member of a class of beings, namely, the class of human beings. The term "class", in this context, does not mean a specific social stratum, but a totality or a set.

Instead of a "member", we could also speak of an "element". A class in this sense is the totality of entities that share a common property. The class of human beings, for example, is the totality of those entities that share the property of being human. We can refer to such a class either in the plural or in the singular. We can say, "Human beings are living beings" or "*The* human being is a living being". An individual human being – say, Socrates – is something concrete and visible. The class of human beings, in contrast, is something abstract, that is, something that has been "drawn out" from the individual, concrete human beings and is no longer visible. Thus, we have never seen that abstract property which is common to all human beings – namely, the property of being human. What we have seen are only individual human beings.

If Socrates is a human being, he is an element in the class of human beings. If, moreover, a human being is a living being, the class of human beings is included in the class of living beings. In the first case, the term "is" indicates (a) an "element relation", in the second case, (b) a "class inclusion relation". The difference is that in a "class inclusion relation", the characteristics of the smaller class are the same as those of the larger class. For example, if the class of living beings is invisible, that of human beings will be so, too. However, in those cases where an element belongs to a class, the properties of the class are not necessarily also properties of the element. For example, while the class of human beings does not have a head, Socrates has one. We can further say that Socrates is Socrates. In this case, the copulative "is" means the same thing as (c) "is identical with".[1] Thus, the word "is" has an existential meaning and at least three copulative meanings – that is, it has at least four different meanings.

Now, although "is" has four different meanings, this does not entail that it simply means four different things, in the sense of being homonymous. A homonym is a word that conveys a variety of meanings, while sounding and being spelt the same. Thus, to give just one example, a "lock" can refer to a device for securing doors or to a bundle of hair. But "is" does not mean a number of different things in this sense. Rather, it has a primary meaning to which the various other meanings are subordinated.

But what is the primary meaning of "is"? Is it the existential meaning or one of the three copulative meanings? It seems to me that it is the existential meaning. To make a proposition such as "Socrates is a human being"

---

1 These three distinctions, as well as the distinction between property and attribute, were worked out by Frege, cf. Concept and Object, pp. 167-178. Transl. Geach and Black. This result has been confirmed by Angelleli, 2015.

true, we must assume that Socrates exists. If Socrates did not exist, the proposition would not be true. Therefore, a true proposition must have a referent in reality, even if the existence of this referent, this human being we call Socrates, is only hypothetical. We could ask "Did Socrates exist?"[2] Likewise, the truth of a proposition such as "The human being is a living being" presupposes the existence of a class, and the truth of "Socrates is Socrates" the existence of Socrates.

This is a law of logic, which can be stated as follows: If a proposition is true, it presupposes the existence of something about which it states a truth. This is also called the law of existential generalisation. The truth of a proposition leads to the general conclusion that there is something to which the proposition applies.

The copulative meaning of "is", then, in this logical sense, presupposes the existential meaning. Therefore, we may assume that, of the four meanings of "is", the existential one is logically fundamental. Although the four meanings of "is" actually vary, these meanings are not disconnected from one another. Rather, the various copulative meanings of "is" are oriented towards *one* basic meaning, so to speak, which is their focus. The term "is" has *one* focal meaning,[3] namely, the meaning of existence. While this was first noted by Aristotle, he did not yet distinguish between the different meanings of "is" mentioned above. Aristotle refers to the focus of the different meanings of "is" not as existence, but rather as substance.[4] The term "substance", in the way Aristotle uses it, can also be translated as essence.

The theory of "what is" is also called the theory of being or ontology. The Greek participle "*on*" means "what is" and the Greek noun "*logos*" also means "theory" or "study". The subject matter of ontology was first described by Aristotle in the following programmatic terms:

> There is a science which investigates being as being and the attributes which belong to this in virtue of its own nature. Now this is not the same as any of the so-called special sciences; for none of these others deals generally with being as being. They cut off a part of being and investigate the attribute of this part; this is what the mathematical sciences for instance do.[5]

---

2 This question was asked by Kleve, 1987.

3 Expression introduced by Owen, 1960, pp. 163-190, esp. pp. 179-190.

4 Cf. Aristotle, Metaph., Book 4, Chapter 2, 1003a33-b10, Book 7, Chapter 1, 1028a13-30. Transl. Ross, rev. Barnes.

5 Metaph., Book 1, Chapter 1, 1003a21-26. Transl. Ross, rev. Barnes.

Thus, the other sciences, such as mathematics, physics or biology, are partial sciences. They "cut off" a part from the whole and they explore what is only insofar as it is countable, moveable or alive. In contrast, ontology does not "cut off" anything from the whole, but rather explores what is insofar as it is. For this reason, it is not a partial or special science, but the science of what is common to all that is. All that is is. Thus, being is common to all that is. Consequently, ontology, as the theory of being as being, is not a special discipline, but a universal one. It is the theory of everything that is, insofar as it is, and, since the existential meaning of "is" is primary, the fundamental question of ontology is: "What exists?"

2. *Real Existence and Real Facts*

The most obvious answer to the question "What exists?" is probably "everything that can be perceived through the senses". Stones, plants, animals and human beings can be perceived by means of our senses. Therefore, we attribute real existence to them. We learnt in the last chapter that real existence, too, is only hypothetical. Nevertheless, with this qualification, we can attribute reality to everything that we experience through our senses, and, for the sake of simplicity, we can describe hypothetical real existence as real existence.

In line with everyday understanding, we define real existence as an existence that can be verified by sensory experience. We have all seen stones, plants, animals and human beings. This is why we say that stones, plants, animals and human beings exist. If we were asked whether stones, plants, animals and human beings really exist, we would answer "Of course they do". For what could be more real than something we can see and touch? We all have carried stones, mowed lawns, petted cats and hugged human beings. The criterion of real existence is our ability to experience things through our senses.

But this criterion does not mean that only that which we actually experience through our senses really exists. At the bottom of the sea, there may be many treasures that nobody has seen. Nevertheless, they really exist, because they may one day be seen and brought to the surface by a diver. Perception through the senses as the criterion of existence means that only what we *can* perceive through our senses really exists. Conversely, what we *cannot* perceive through the senses has no real existence. We have never seen a winged horse, except in paintings. But a painted horse is not a real horse. A painted horse has no real existence, except perhaps as part of a canvas. Therefore, the criterion of what really exists is also the criterion of what does not really exist.

What really exists exists in connection with other things. While this connection can come about in various ways, each of these ways is restricted by *categories*. Category (from the Greek *katēgoría*) literally means an accusation, but also means a statement. We can state that Socrates is a certain height, say, 5 foot 6. His height falls under the category of quantity. We can state that he has a certain shape, that he is stout, for example. Girth falls under the category of quality. We can also state that at a certain time, he is in a certain place, say, at 7:00 am in the marketplace in Athens. Place and time fall under the categories of space and time. We can further state that he is doing something, for example, that he is walking around "barefoot",[6] or that he is undergoing something, such as freezing because he is wearing nothing but a sheepskin. Walking around and freezing fall under the category of acting and undergoing. We can state that he has certain relationships with other people, for example, that he is married to Xanthippe and has three sons. Being married and having children fall under the category of relationships. Finally, we can state that he is a human being. This is the category of essence, insofar as it says what he is.

"Essence" is an ambiguous term. It has both a concrete and an abstract meaning. The concrete essence is the concrete Socrates, that is, Socrates in the flesh and blood. The abstract essence, on the other hand, is what is left of Socrates once all of the flesh and blood has been "abstracted" away, that is, removed from the concrete Socrates. What is then left behind is what he has in common with all other human beings. Ultimately, this is the bare fact of his humanity. The term "substance" is as ambiguous as the term "essence". Like essence, substance can be either concrete or abstract. Concrete substance is the result of the coalescence of matter and form. Abstract substance is what is left over, once matter has been eliminated. The division of what really exists into categories also goes back to Aristotle.[7]

The precise number of categories identified by Aristotle is controversial. But what is decisive is his realisation that things that exist, exist in combination with other things that exist. The way in which things that exist can exist in combination with other things is predetermined by these categories. Categories are, on the one hand, the most universal concepts under which the predicates of a simple proposition fall. A simple proposition is one that consists of a subject, a predicate and, perhaps, an object. A sim-

6 Cf. Plato, Phdr. 229 a.

7 Cf. Aristotle, Cat., On the category of substance, Chapter 5, 2b11-4b19.

ple proposition is not composed of multiple clauses, but it can become part of a composite statement. But categories are not only the most universal concepts under which the predicates of a simple proposition fall. They are also the most universal genres under which things identified by linguistic predicates can be classified.[8] They are the largest "drawers" in which we can "store" almost everything that is.

Today, the combinations of things that exist within categories are also called facts. For example, it is a fact that Mr or Mrs Smith is so and so tall and has such and such a shape, happens to be in a specific place at a specific time, does or undergoes something, or is a father or a mother. When we talk about a fact, we do not say that it "is", but rather that it "is the case". Since the world consists not only of individual beings, but also of combinations of beings, it is a sign of progress in thinking that Wittgenstein introduces his *Tractatus Logico-Philosophicus* with these words: "The world is everything that is the case. The world is the totality of facts, not of things."[9]

A thing is, or exists, while a fact is the case. A thing is something that is; a fact is a combination of things that are. The combinations of things that are occur within the framework of certain possibilities. The possible combinations are limited by categories. We cannot connect willy-nilly anything with anything else. For example, we cannot say that Socrates is a prime number. That would be a *category mistake*, since the essence of Socrates does not fall under the category of either quantity or number. Likewise, we cannot say that Mr Smith or Mrs Jones is a square root, because the essence of neither Mr Smith nor Mrs Jones falls under the category of square roots, except perhaps in a figurative sense. Thus, the world is the totality of facts insofar as the world is everything that is organised into categories. Now we can formulate the question "What exists?" more accurately as "What facts are the case?"

3. *Physical Facts and Psychic Facts*

The first facts that come to mind in asking what facts are the case are probably those that we can verify by means of the evidence of our external senses, for example, the fact that snow is white. This is a physical fact. We do

8 Cf. Aristotle, e.g. Metaph., Book 5, Chapter 6, 1016b32, Book 10, Chapter 13, 1054b35.

9 TLP, § 1 and § 1.1. Transl. Ogden.

not see *the fact that* snow is white with our eyes, but rather see the *whiteness of* the snow – or rather, to put it more accurately, only the white colour of, say, a particular snowball. The sense of sight, which provides evidence for this contention, is directed towards the outside. It, like the other four senses, is an external sense. Let us call facts that we can verify by means of the evidence provided by our external senses "*physical facts*". We have learnt that physical facts – such as snow is white – are also hypothetical (cf. pp. 87-88). However, subject to this qualification of being hypothetical, we can simplify matters by calling physical facts real, even if they are real only in a hypothetical sense.

Yet, we cannot supply evidence for all facts through our external senses. For example, I can see the white colour of the snow, but I cannot see the *process of seeing* itself. Nevertheless, it is an actual fact that I can see a white snowball, hear the whistling of a marmot, smell the odour of a cigar, taste the juice of a lemon and feel for the key to my front door. It is further an actual fact that I feel pain, say, if I am stung by a wasp. I can just about see the sting of the wasp, but the pain itself I can neither see nor perceive with any of my other external senses. However, since I nonetheless feel the pain, the evidence for the facts in question is supplied, not by my external perception, but by my internal or inner perception. Like external perception, inner perception requires the stimulation of my nerve endings. To borrow a somewhat dramatic image from one of my students: "The breakers of the world crash against the cliffs of my body."

Facts for which we can supply evidence solely by means of our inner perception we will call "*psychic facts*". We can also call them "facts of consciousness". Consciousness is another concept that cannot be explicitly defined, but only elucidated. The concept of consciousness comprises everything that can occur in consciousness, for example, faculties of consciousness.

Yet, consciousness contains a variety of faculties. Accordingly, philosophers and psychologists have divided consciousness in various ways. In everyday life, we still speak, for example, about feeling, willing and thinking. Since it is not clear how these different faculties of the soul relate to each other, the pattern I find most illuminating is the one introduced by Descartes, the founder of the modern philosophy of consciousness, in his *Meditations on First Philosophy* and adopted by Franz Brentano (1838-1911) in his *Psychology from an Empirical Standpoint*. Descartes distinguishes between (a) ideas, (b) judgments and (c) acts of will,[10] and Brentano follows

10 Descartes, Meditations, Meditation 3, Section 5, pp. 36-37. Transl. Cottingham.

him by distinguishing (a) representations, (b) judgments and (c) acts of will, which he also calls motions of the soul, interests, or acts of love and hate.[11]

The term "idea" here means the same as representation (*Vorstellung*). But the term "representation" is ambiguous. We can take it to mean either the act of representation or what is being represented, that is, the content of the representation. When we say that representations are a part of consciousness, we mean acts of representation.

An act of representation, again, cannot be explicitly defined, that is, replaced by another term. An act of representation is anything I represent. Therefore, to elucidate, an act of representation is anything that can occur in our consciousness.

A judgment consists in our recognition of a proposition as true or false. Here, we must distinguish between judgment and proposition. A judgment is something psychic and, like a representation, may vary from one person to another. In contrast, a proposition – that is, the content of a sentence (see p. 71) – is not something psychic, but we assume that it remains identical despite the differences between the psychic processes of different people. Thus, we may or may not recognise Pythagoras' theorem as true, but the sense of the sentence "$a^2 + b^2 = c^2$", that is, the proposition $a^2 + b^2 = c^2$, is true regardless.

An act of will consists in our desiring something as good or avoiding it as bad.

According to this Cartesian model, consciousness has different levels: The lowest level is that of representations, the second level is that of judgments and the third level is that of acts of will. Judgments require representations. Acts of will require both judgments and representations. Without representations, I cannot regard anything as either true or false or desire anything as good or bad. Likewise, without judgment, that is, without evaluating something as good or bad, I cannot desire it as good or reject it as bad. If I desire an apple, I do so because I have explicitly or tacitly passed the judgment that it is good. If I avoid milk that has gone off, I do so because I have explicitly or tacitly passed the judgment that it is bad. As a rule, we do not desire or avoid "blindly", but rather do so while "seeing", and this is precisely because our response is based on a judgment. Yet, this judgment need not always be explicit or pronounced. We sometimes find certain people appealing or unappealing, pleasant or unpleasant, "at first

11 Brentano, Psychology II, Chapter 6, § 3, pp. 33-36. Transl. Rancurello et al.

sight". As Shakespeare put it: "Who ever lov'd, that lov'd not at first sight?"[12]

What is the case in our consciousness is a fact of consciousness in the broader sense. A pronounced judgment, on the other hand, is a fact of consciousness in the narrower sense. Naturally, we are not conscious, in the narrower sense, of all facts of consciousness in the broader sense. I may see a face in a crowd without consciously registering it. I may only become conscious of my having seen that face before when I see it again later. It is an astonishing property of human beings – acquired in the course of evolution – that we are able to remember faces, as opposed to masks or names. Similarly, I may feel a pain without becoming conscious of it because it has not reached the intensity that would draw my attention to it. Only a stronger pain is a fact of consciousness in the narrower sense. So Nietzsche proclaims: "One burns something in so that it remains in the memory. Only something which never ceases to *cause pain* stays in the memory."[13]

I can affirm a proposition even without knowing explicitly that I am doing so. Any child who accuses his or her mother of contradicting herself tacitly affirms the axiom of non-contradiction. In his *Confessions*, Augustine reports: "I have personally watched and studied a jealous baby. It could not yet speak and, pale with jealousy and bitterness, glared at its brother sharing its mother's milk."[14] Although the infant has no word for and probably no concept of jealousy, it seems to harbour jealous feelings of which it is not aware. The child mentioned by Sigmund Freud in *The Interpretation of Dreams* also seems to be unconsciously jealous. Freud writes: "So far the child has been the only one; now he is informed that the stork has brought a new baby. The child inspects the new arrival, and expresses his opinion with decision: 'The stork had better take it back again!'"[15]

We adults can also be swayed by motives of which we are not conscious. We may think that we are trying to help, but all we want is to steal the limelight. Conversely, we may think that we are acting out of a desire for recognition, but we are obeying purer motives than we ourselves believe. An act of will, that is, an act of consciousness in the wider sense, can be carried out without being accompanied by an act of consciousness in the

12 As You Like It, Act III, Scene 5, Phoebe.

13 Nietzsche, Genealogy, Treatise 2, § 3, p. 311. Transl. Kaufman and Hollingdale with modifications. Emphasis and quotation marks without reference in the original.

14 St Augustine, Confessions, Book 1, Section 7, Subsection 11. Transl. Chadwick.

15 Freud, Interpretation of Dreams, Book 5, Chapter D, Section d, p. 213. Transl. Brill, p. 299. Quoted without footnote.

narrower sense. On the map of our soul – as Kant put it in his *Anthropology from a Pragmatic Point of View* – only a few places are illuminated: "Thus, the field of *obscure* representations is the largest in the human being."[16]

A representation is obscure when it is not articulated in language. If on the map of our soul there are only a few places that are illuminated, it does not follow that there are no other places that *could* be illuminated. Nor does it follow that, if we were not conscious of a conscious act, we would be unable to articulate it. Just as there are things that I cannot perceive with my external senses, there are also acts of consciousness of which I am not conscious. At first sight, this seems to be a contradiction.

The contradiction is resolved if we say that a fact of consciousness in the broader sense need not be conscious to us in the narrower sense. But it must have the potential to become conscious. It will become conscious *if* we articulate it in language. But just as there are more physical facts than we articulate, there are also more psychic ones.

Leibniz goes so far as to say: "But a soul can read in itself only what is distinctly represented there; it cannot unfold all its folds at once, because they go to infinity."[17] But, in order to show that the unopened folds of the soul "go to infinity", we would need to articulate them in such a way that the articulation could continue indefinitely. How could we account for something that we are unable to articulate? In principle, having learnt language, we should be able to express whatever we can imagine; otherwise, we would not be able to imagine it.

This is also called the principle of expressibility.[18] Alternatively, we can call it the principle of articulability. According to this principle, it should be possible to articulate unconscious "knowledge". But, articulating what I unconsciously "know" is not as easy as opening a closed fist. Every teacher has experienced how difficult it is, not only for children, but also for adults, to express what they already "know" at an unconscious level. Every child "knows" what milk tastes like. But can the child say what it tastes like? We all "know" what a piano sounds like. But can we say what it sounds like? Likewise, we all "know" unconsciously what the word "is" means. But to put that unconscious knowledge into language is very difficult.

For physical facts, we can supply evidence from our external perception. For psychic facts, we can do so from our internal perception. We can call

16 Anthropology, AA, Vol. 7, § 5, p. 136. Transl. Loudon.

17 Leibniz, Monadology, § 61. Transl. Arlew and Garber.

18 Searle, Speech Acts, Part 1, Chapter 1, Section 5.

both kinds of fact real, because we are able to provide evidence for both from our perception. This world view, which recognises two kinds of fact, that is, physical and psychic, is often called dualistic. It is a view that goes back in modern times to Descartes, who claims in his *Meditations on the First Philosophy* that human beings consist of two things, extension and thought.[19] The extended thing is the body; the thinking thing is consciousness. I can experience my body through the intermediary of my external perception and my consciousness directly through my inner perception. But first I am directed outward. It is only when I turn back to myself that I experience my inner being.

It would seem now that physical facts are more real than psychic ones. It would seem that snow being white is more real than my seeing the white colour of snow. The external world would seem to be more real than any inner world. Yet, Descartes shows us that this is not so. It is actually easier for me to doubt all external perception than it is for me to doubt my inner perception. It is easier for me to doubt that snow is white than to doubt that I see the white colour of snow. As we have seen, sensory evidence offers only a prima facie criterion of truth. If, according to Descartes, "it is prudent never to trust wholly those who have deceived us even once",[20] we can infer from a single case of deception by our senses that they could deceive us again.

Internal perception, then, seems less deceptive than external perception. In Shakespeare's *Hamlet*, Polonius reads out a letter from Hamlet to Ophelia: "Doubt that stars are fire,/ Doubt that the sun doth move,/ Doubt truth to be a liar. / But never doubt I love."[21] Hamlet is more certain of his love than of the sun and stars. He could say, along with Prince Klemens von Metternich, "Of all realities the strongest for me is love." That the sun moves and the stars are fire could be a mere dream – as could the whiteness of the snow. Even then, however, we would be performing acts of consciousness, precisely in the form of dreaming. Psychic facts seem more real than physical ones, since we can doubt the existence of the latter more readily than the existence of the former. The existence of physical facts is, therefore, more hypothetical than that of psychic ones.

Following Descartes, Brentano writes: "However, besides the fact that it has a special object, inner perception possesses another distinguishing

---

19 Descartes, Meditations, 2nd Meditation, cf. esp. Sections 5, 8, 19-20, 23. Transl. Cottingham.

20 Descartes, Meditations, 1st Meditation, Section 3, 9. Transl. Cottingham.

21 Act II, Scene 2.

characteristic: its immediate, infallible self-evidence. Of all the types of knowledge of the objects of experience, inner perception alone possesses this characteristic."[22] This is true, if only in the sense that the evidence of inner perception is *less* deceptive than the evidence of external evidence. Nevertheless, the "immediate, infallible" evidence of inner perception is also merely prima facie evidence. We can not only be mistaken about our own feelings for other people – for example, love – but we can also doubt a sensation, like the sensation of pain, because we are capable of imagining pain.

But now a further objection arises: Could we not reduce the psychic facts to physical ones, so that we would be left with only *one* kind of fact, the physical? We would then no longer be dealing with a dualistic picture of the world, but with a monistic, physicalist one. Is it not the case that psychic facts are, as it were, only garments of the physical ones? After all, every representation, every judgment, every act of the will is nothing but a cerebral process. This assumption marks the beginning of the great modern programme of research into the naturalisation of consciousness.

When it comes to the naturalisation of consciousness, there have been similar developments in modern science, where, for example, the phlogiston theory of combustion has been replaced with the oxidation theory. According to the former theory, combustible bodies contain a certain substance (phlogiston) that escapes in the process of combustion. According to the latter theory, the air itself contains a combustible part, called "flammable air", which is, in fact, oxygen. Thus, it seems possible to replace the pre-scientific "phlogiston" of psychic fact with a certain kind of physical fact. Just as some phenomena perceived through our external senses appear different to us from their physical nature – after all, we do not perceive colours and sounds as light waves and sound waves – so certain cerebral processes appear to us only as psychic facts. Psychic facts, then, only seem to have a psychic existence. In reality, they are nothing but physical facts.

However, it cannot be said that this programme of naturalising consciousness has been a success. The reason for this is not that the science of the human brain is insufficiently advanced. Rather, it has to do with something more fundamental, that is, conceptual. Leibniz voiced the following objection in this regard:

---

22 Brentano, Psychology I, Book 2, § 6, 128. Transl. Rancurello, Terrelland and McAlister.

> Moreover, it must be confessed that perception and that which depends upon it are inexplicable on mechanical grounds, that is to say, by means of figures and motions. And supposing there were a machine, so constructed as to think, feel, and have perception, it might be conceived as increased in size, while keeping the same proportions, so that one might go into it as into a mill. That being so, we should, on examining its interior, find only parts which work one upon another, and never anything by which to explain a perception.[23]

This objection is circular because it presupposes what it tries to prove. Nevertheless, it illustrates something peculiar about representations. A representation, that is, something psychic, cannot be explained by something physical, because the psychic is conceptually different from the physical. Facts are facts. Yet, the evidence for physical facts is in the public domain, while the evidence for psychic facts is accessible only to me. The evidence for physical facts is given to me through the mediation of the external senses, the evidence for psychic facts directly through internal perception. Having an inner perception means possessing an internal perspective.[24] In contrast, we perceive physical facts only from the outside. Therefore, if we could reduce psychic facts to physical ones, we would lose some of the conceptual content that we associate with psychic facts, that is, the inner perspective that is specific to psychic facts. Any reductionist explanation that says, for example, "Acts of representation are nothing but cerebral processes," could be countered by asking: "An act of representation may be nothing but a corresponding cerebral process, but is the corresponding cerebral process an act of representation?"

I would answer this question in the negative because we cannot exhaust the concept of the psychic by using physical criteria. Perhaps we can localise a cerebral process if, say, we feel pain. But the pain itself is not a localisable part of the cerebral cortex. Also, the pain is accessible only to me. Only my behaviour while I am in pain, like the relevant part of the cerebral cortex, is accessible to everybody. Yet, my strained facial expression, like a part of my cerebral cortex, is not perceived from the inside, but from the outside.

We can localise a cerebral process and even measure eye movements when we dream. But nobody else can perceive my dreams as I do. Others can only perceive an account of my dreams. In doing so, however, they do not

23 Leibniz, Monadology, § 17. Transl. Arlew and Garber.

24 This has been made clear once more by Nagel, 1974, pp. 435-450.

perceive my dreams from the inside, but only from the outside, because what they hear are the words I use to tell my dreams. Thus, Wittgenstein's remark, "An 'inner process' stands in need of outward criteria",[25] is correct. But no external criterion can exhaust the meaning we associate with the concept of an "inner process". Because of this conceptual irreducibility of the psychic to the physical, we cannot entirely dismiss this dualistic world picture.

4. *Semantic Existence and Semantic Facts*

There is a further kind of existence, which we cannot describe as real because we cannot provide any evidence for it, either through our external or our internal perceptions. For example, we all assume that there are such things as numbers and combinations of numbers. Thus, we all believe that there is the number 1 and the combination 1+1=2. What we can perceive through our senses are only materialised numerals, for example, the numerals on our watch. But if we say 1+1=2, we do not mean that the numeral "1" on our wristwatch, joined to the numeral "1", results in the numeral "2". The numeral "1", joined to the numeral "1", would only result in the numeral "11". Rather, we mean that the meaning of the numeral "1", added to the meaning of the numeral "1", results in the meaning of the numeral "2". We obviously assume that the numerals "1" and "2" have a meaning. The meaning of the numeral "1" is the number 1, the meaning of the numeral "2" is the number 2, and so on. It is only to the meaning that we ascribe an existence when we say that there is a number 1 or that 1+1=2 is true.

We further ascribe existence to classes, for example, the class of human beings, which I mentioned before. Classes can also be combined. If, for example, we say "The human being is a living being", the class of human beings is included in the class of living beings.

According to a hypothesis championed by Whitehead and Russell in *Principia Mathematica*, numbers are classes of classes.[26] The number 1 would be the class of all unit classes, the number 2 the class of all two-membered classes, the number 3 the class of all three-membered classes, and so on. A unit class [x] is the class that contains x as the sole element. It must be distinguished from the element x because it has at least one property that the

25 Wittgenstein, PI, § 580. Transl. Anscombe et al.

26 Cf. PM, Part II, Section A, § 52.

element does not have, that is, it contains an element. The class of all unit classes is the class of all classes that contain x as the only element. The class of all two-membered classes is the class of all classes that contain x and y as the only elements, where $x \neq y$. The class of all three-membered classes is the class of all classes that contain x, y and z as the only elements, where $x \neq y \neq z$, and so on.

What kind of existence do classes and classes of classes have? Obviously, nobody has ever seen, heard, tasted, felt or smelled a class or a class of classes. Classes cannot be experienced though our external perception. They have, in this sense, no real existence.

But can they perhaps be experienced through inner perception? A possible answer, attributed to Plato, is that we grasp invisible things, such as classes, not with our bodily eyes, but with our "mind's eye". This "eye of the soul" is an intellect that does not infer, but that, like our bodily eye, is supposed to have the ability to see things directly. However, what it sees is not the visible, but the invisible. The paradox of how we can "see" the invisible seems to be resolved as follows: We see the invisible not with our bodily eyes, but with our mind's eye. If these invisible entities have no *real* existence, they nevertheless have an *ideal* existence. So Plato writes: "Ungenerated and indestructible", "admitting no modification", "imperceptible to sight or the other senses", they are "what thinking is determined to see."[27]

Now the hypothesis of a mind's eye is a wonderful image of how we perceive things for the existence of which we cannot produce any sensory evidence through external experience. But granting any reality to the image would impose a burden of proof on us that we would hardly be able to meet. Even our bodily eyes do not perceive things directly, but rather see things as something particular (cf. p. 42). Why should what is true of bodily eyes not also be true of the mind's eye?

Further, to repeat what Wittgenstein said, an "internal process", such as an intellectual vision or intuition, needs external criteria. But what external criterion could there be for an "intellectual intuition" of my own? If I have such an experience, I cannot show its existence to others (who do not have it and who do not believe in it) by means of an external criterion. If others have it, and I do not, they also cannot show it to me by means of an external criterion. The hypothesis of an intellectual intuition can be neither verified nor falsified in an intersubjective way. Such a hypothesis is accessible to introspection alone and is thus of a private nature. This leaves the arbitrariness of the observer with substantial room for manoeuvre. While the

27 Ti. 51 a. My translation.

wings of intellectual vision may raise us above reality and above most our fellow human beings, do they not also resemble the wings with which the seraphims cover their faces?[28]

If I were to claim to have a special vision that others do not have, I would hardly be able to convince those who had not had it. If anything could convince them, it would be their belief in an authority. An intellectual vision is a metaphorical auxiliary construction to explain the paradox that we can "see" things that we cannot see. However, to infer from the metaphor of an intellectual vision the reality of that vision *and* of these invisible things would be a mistake. Thus, both intellectual and sensory vision must be ruled out as means of registering invisible classes.

How, then, do we register the invisible? Actually, Plato probably knew that this intellectual vision was a metaphor when he wrote that only the best soul "which following God becomes most like to him"[29] can see the invisible in a "place beyond heaven",[30] but even that soul sees it only "with difficulty".[31] He also wrote: "Immaterial things which are the noblest and greatest, are only shown clearly through *logos*, and in no other way."[32]

The word "*logos*" literally means "speech", but in Plato it can also mean "explanation", "definition" or "argument". If the only way to reveal "the noblest and greatest" things clearly is through *logos*, this can only happen clearly through speech, explanation, definition or argument and not through either sensory or intellectual vision.

Here I will take the literal meaning of "*logos*" as my starting point: "The human being" as indicating the class of human beings or "numbers" as indicating classes of classes are abstract nouns. By means of language, we are able to create any number of abstract nouns. We can do this, for example, by converting adjectives into nouns and giving them the status of subjects. We can take the adjective "red" and make up the abstract noun "redness" and, in doing so, give redness the status of a subject. Likewise, we can turn the adjective "white" into the noun "whiteness" and give whiteness the status of a subject. Then, instead of saying "Snow is white", we could say "Snow contains whiteness". If we then formulate true propositions about

28 Cf. Isaiah, VI, 2, King James Bible: "Above it stood the seraphims each one had **six** wings; with twain he covered his face."

29 Phdr. 248 a. My translation.

30 Ibid. My translation.

31 Phdr. 247 c. My translation of *mogis*.

32 Plt. 286 a. Transl. Jowett modified. For this passage, as well as an interpretation of intellectual vision and the "light in the soul" in Plato, cf. my little book, 2007, pp. 47-51 and pp. 106-120.

such abstract subjects – for example, "Whiteness is a colour", "The human being is a living being" or "1+1=2" – we assume, according to the law of existential generalisation, that there are subjects such as the class of whiteness, the class of human beings and the class of all unit classes or all two-membered classes, etc.

However, these abstract subjects do not exist in the real world, but only in our way of representing the real world in abstractions by giving – with the help of our language – abstract nouns the status of subjects. Abstract subjects are of course not linguistic phenomena in the same way as nouns are, if we regard them as mere strings of sounds or letters. Yet, they are linguistic phenomena insofar as they are meanings of nouns. What, then, is left if abstract subjects have no real existence? Obviously, the meanings of abstract nouns.

Even a sceptic who believes that abstract nouns have no meaning would nonetheless still assume that these nouns have meaning. In order to be able to say, for example, that the abstract noun "human being" has no meaning, he would still have to assume an interpersonal meaning for that noun. The meaning of nouns is the subject matter of semantics. Therefore, abstract nouns have no real, but only semantic, existence.[33]

Real existence is an existence that can be verified by the evidence of external or internal sense perception. Semantic existence, as I define it, is the existence attributed to the meaning of an expression – the meaning of "human being" in "The human being is a living being" or the meaning of the numeral "1" in "1+1=2" – which, in the absence of a referent that can be

33 The term "semantic existence" is introduced in my paper *Normatives 'ist', Sein Gottes und Leibniz-Schellingsche Frage*, pp. 390-391. The distinction I make there between real and semantic existence roughly corresponds to that between "exist" (*hypárchein*) and "subsist" (*hyphístasthai*), represented by the Stoics (cf. SVF, vol. II, fr. 322, fr. 488, fr. 541) and still in the 20th century by Russell (cf. Problems, Chapter 9), but I try to define the concept of subsistence more precisely by means of Frege's theory of the sense becoming the referent. Quine objects to the distinction between two meanings of "there is", stating that "the distinction between one meaning of 'there is' for concrete objects and another for abstract ones – given only one sense of 'there is' for both – makes no sense", Word and Object, § 49, p. 242. Quine seems to assume that the concept of being can explicitly be defined by "only one sense of 'there is'" and that it is the genus of which the being of concrete things and the being of abstract things are species. However, I am not saying that the concept of being can be explicitly defined (cf. p. 129), but only that our *everyday understanding* of being can be implicitly elucidated by means of the distinction between real and semantic existence. But, in an implicit definition or elucidation, the definiendum may recur in the definiens.

experienced in reality, itself becomes the referent. With this definition, I am extending Frege's apt remark (that "the indirect reference of a word is accordingly its customary sense"[34]) to cover abstract nouns. The "indirect reference of a word", in Frege's terminology, means the referent of a word in indirect speech. In indirect speech, I speak about the speech of another. If, for example, I say "A man named John told me that he was at home", my indirect reference is to the fact that John is at home. My direct reference, on the other hand, is to John's telling me that he is at home.

The same principle applies to abstract objects, where the object is not an object in the external world but rather the meaning of the expression in question. For example, if we say "The human being is a living being", the noun "human being" does not refer to a specific individual in the external world (say, a woman named Sarah), but rather to the meaning of "human being" in this particular sentence. Similarly, by saying "The class of human beings is included in that of living beings", we do not refer to a specific fact in the external world, but rather to the content of that sentence. The content of a sentence is also called a proposition. By means of such a sentence, therefore, we refer to a proposition.

But if we say "1+1=2", the term "1" no longer refers to a specific thing – say, a single stone – in the external world, but to the meaning of the term "1". Likewise, if we say "1+1=2", we are no longer referring to two specific things in the external world. Rather, we are referring to the proposition "1+1=2".

Thus, in such sentences about abstract nouns, the referent is no longer a thing in the real world, but rather the content of the sentence, that is, the proposition itself. We can call this the reification of propositions, which turns them into facts.

Naturally, we cannot see this referent, or this combination of referents, either with our bodily eyes or with the mind's eye. If we nonetheless say that these referents exist, we are asserting that the meanings of the corresponding expressions, or the contents of the corresponding sentences, exist. Propositions such as "The class of human beings is included in that of living beings" or "1+1=2" are not real facts. However, since it is still the case that the class of human beings is included in the class of living beings, and that 1+1 equals 2, we can still talk about facts. Yet, they are not *real* but rather *semantic facts*. By the act of linguistic reference to such facts, the meanings of the expressions themselves are *made* into facts.

---

34 Frege, Sinn and Bedeutung, p. 145. Transl. Geach and Black with modification, Beaney, p. 154.

Thus, semantic existence, unlike real existence, is an artificial one, created by human beings. Semantic facts are manufactured facts. They are the reified rules for the use of abstract expressions. Once we have turned them into facts, these meanings, or combinations of meanings, gain a status that is analogous to that of natural facts – but only an analogous status, for these semantic facts have no real existence. Nevertheless, once we have turned them into facts, they exist *as if* they were to be found in reality. They exist *as if* they were wholly independent of the circumstance that they only came into being thanks to the human ability to create the relevant abstract terms.

Once they have gained this seemingly independent status, it is possible to forget their human origin and to believe that they are really independent. This origin being forgotten, it might be asked where they exist and how they can be perceived. Since these meanings or combinations of meanings cannot be found in the empirical world or be perceived through our external senses, some philosophers – called Platonists – hit upon the idea that the "home" of these meanings or combinations of meaning was in an invisible world that we could see only with the mind's eye. Plato, however, seems to have known that such ethereal things can clearly be shown only by speech, explanation or definition "and in no other way". At least he lets proclaim that the mind's vision of these ethereal beings is attached to speech or occurs "always with true *logos*".[35]

Thus, in addition to real facts – whether physical or psychic – we have to reckon with semantic facts. There can be as many of these as there are reifiable meanings. Since these meanings are not verifiable by internal or external experience, they can be multiplied indefinitely. The realm of semantic facts is limited only by the rule that they must not logically contradict themselves. We may not only assume that there is the class of all unit classes, two-membered classes and three-membered classes, but we may also assume that there is the class of all four- or five-membered classes, etc., extending all the way to the class of that class which contains an infinity of elements. With Cantor, we may even assume an infinity of classes of classes that again contain an infinity of elements. But no intellectual intuition is able to visualise an infinity of classes with an infinity of elements. Classes and hierarchies of classes have semantic existence only because we can meaningfully talk about them.

A round square, on the other hand, does not even have semantic existence, because a round square is not something that we can meaningfully talk

35 Ti. 51 e.

about. A round square is not a square. The corresponding expression "round square" therefore has no possible referent either in the real or in the semantic world, except in a figurative sense when we say that we have to round a square or to square a circle. In this case, we mean that we have to face not an impossible, but a very difficult task. For semantic existence, Hilbert's criterion of existence, that is, non-contradiction (cf. p. 64), is a necessary and sufficient criterion, whereas for real existence, it is only a necessary criterion, but not a sufficient one.

A contradictory concept like a round square is, in distinction to an imaginary or fictional entity like a golden mountain, merely a chimeric entity.[36] It exists neither in the real nor in the semantic world, but only in words. It has therefore only a verbal existence.

Since semantic objects can, in principle, be multiplied at will, some philosophers conceived the idea that they should not be allowed to proliferate. William of Ockham (c. 1285-1347) coined the maxim: "Entities should not be multiplied unnecessarily."

5. *The Being of Universals, the Being of Fictitious Things and the Being of Nothingness*

a) The Being of Universals

The concept of semantic existence allows us to address the so-called problem of universals. Aristotle defines the universal as "that which is by its nature predicated of a number of things".[37] Therefore, since the meanings of nouns refer to several particular things, the meanings of universal nouns are also universal. For example, when we say that Socrates is a human being, that Plato is a human being, that Aristotle is a human being, etc., the

36 I refer here with modification to Spinoza: *Metaphysical Thoughts* 1.3.4: "*Chimaeras properly called verbal beings*: First, it should be noted that we may properly call a Chimaera a verbal being [*ens verbale*] because it is neither in the intellect nor in the imagination. For it cannot be expressed except in words. E.g., we can, indeed, express a square Circle in words, but we cannot imagine it in any way, much less understand it. So a Chimaera is nothing but a word, and impossibility cannot be numbered among the affections of being, for it is only a negation" (transl. Curley). But semantic existence encompasses much more than what can be imagined, that is, all that of which we can speak without contradiction, e.g. an infinity of classes of classes that again contain an infinity of elements.

37 De int., Chapter. 7, 17a38. Transl. Ackrill.

meaning of the universal noun "human being" applies to several individuals. Not only are nouns, such as human being, house, etc., universal, but adjectives (which may denote either properties or relationships) are as well. We can say, for example, that Socrates is a certain degree smaller and older than Plato, that Plato is a certain degree taller and older than Aristotle, that Aristotle is a certain degree taller and older than his pupil Theophrastus, etc. The words "smaller", "taller" and "older" are used in relation to several different men. In fact, not only nouns and adjectives but all verbs, pronouns and prepositions are things of which there are or may be many instances. Thus, most of the words in our sentences, except proper names, are universals. The problem of universals has to do with the way in which this common element exists. Porphyry (232-305), in his *Introduction* to Aristotle's theory of categories, formulated the decisive options as follows:

> I shall not say anything about whether genera and species exist as substances, or are confined to mere conceptions; and if they are substances, whether they are material or immaterial; and whether they exist separately from sensible objects, or in them immanently. This sort of problem is very deep, and requires a more extensive investigation.[38]

This notwithstanding, let us venture to say a few words about this problem by means of a short aside, since we are unable to plumb its full depths at this point. Genera and species are classes. Genera constitute the class, species the subclass. In the statement "The human being is a living being", the universal name "human being" denotes the species or the subclass, and the universal name "living being" denotes the genus or the class.

Regarding the mode of existence of universals, Porphyry distinguishes between two possibilities. The first possibility (a) is called realism. It was advocated especially by Plato and Aristotle. According to this position, genera and species really exist, although they obviously do not have bodies. The second (b) is called conceptualism. In modern times, it was championed by, among others, John Locke (1632-1704). According to this position, genera and species exist only in our minds, as thoughts or concepts.

There is also a third position, not mentioned by Porphyry, namely, (c) nominalism. Like conceptualism, nominalism holds that in reality there are only particular things. But, in contrast to conceptualism, nominalism regards genera and species as existing in name only. If names are regarded as nothing but sounds or letters, universals exist only as a *flatus vocis*, that

---

38 Introduction, 1a8-12. Transl. Edghill.

is, a "breath of the voice". But this position is so extreme that – as with the negation of the propositions of identity and non-contradiction – I doubt that anybody has seriously advocated it. According to the nominalist, the universal noun "nominalist" itself would only be a "breath of the voice". And the nominalist's voice would only be able to "breathe" the name of nominalism without making it intelligible either to others or to himself.

In fact, some of the philosophers remembered under the heading of nominalism, for example, Ockham (cf. p. 112), incline towards conceptualism. In contrast, even Quine, who is regarded as a nominalist, assumes the existence of abstract objects (at least as a useful myth) because, he says, "science would be hopelessly crippled without abstract objects".[39] Classes, too, are abstract objects.

Under the first heading of this taxonomy, (a) realism, Porphyry further distinguishes two possibilities: Either (a') the genera and species are separate from bodies or (a'') they exist in, and are dependent on, bodies. The first (a') of these possibilities is Platonic realism about universals; the second (a'') is Aristotelian realism about universals. Thus, we can distinguish between (a) realism about universals, (b) conceptualism about universals and (c) nominalism about universals, with (a) realism being broken down into (a') Platonic and (a'') Aristotelian variants.

According to the Platonic (a') variant, "we usually assume one distinct form for each group of many things to which we apply the same name".[40] "*Eidos*", or "*idea*", rendered here as "form", is Plato's word for what we call universals or classes today. The Platonic ideas exist as independent essences or substances, of which the following predicates are proclaimed (cf. p. 107): They are "ungenerated and indestructible", "admitting no modification", "imperceptible to sight or the other senses", as well as that which "thinking is determined to see".[41]

The Platonic ideas, therefore, are not ideas in today's sense of subjective representations. Rather, they are something objective. Thus, even if there were no individual human beings, the idea of "human being" would exist as "an ungenerated and indestructible" substance. Conversely, the Socrates we see is not an independent and unmodifiable substance, but only a generated and destructible phenomenon that we can perceive with our eyes or in other ways. According to the Aristotelian variant (a''), Plato is right insofar as he assumes the existence of a single idea for the many things to

39 Quine, From Stimulus to Science, Chapter 3, p. 40.
40 R. 596 a. My translation.
41 Ti. 51 a. My translation.

which we apply the same name. It is also Aristotle who explicitly introduces the distinction between genus and species.

For Aristotle, essence or substance is what underlies any given genus and is "neither said of a subject nor in a subject, for example, the individual man or the individual horse".[42] Thus, concrete human beings of flesh and blood fall under the genus of human being. We do not say "The human being is Socrates or Socrates is in the human being", but rather the reverse, that is, "Socrates is a human being and being human is in Socrates". At the same time, genera and species, for Aristotle, are substances only in a secondary or abstract sense.

Unlike Plato, Aristotle does not regard universals as independent entities, but only as dependent predicates: "For it seems impossible that any universal term should be the name of a substance."[43] The first, or concrete, substance is something particular, and only the so-called second, or abstract, substance is something universal. The universal which is said of the particular has no independent existence, but is only a quality of the particular in question. If, for example, we say "Socrates is a human being", we refer to a quality of a particular individual, namely, the quality of being human or the fact of being a member of the species. But being human, or being a member of the species, does not refer to a particular individual, say, the flesh-and-blood Socrates we can see. Rather, it is a quality which distinguishes the human species from others. It is the "occurrence of an essence" in a particular individual.[44] We can mentally perceive this universal quality by inductive abstraction, Thus, we see in the barefoot Socrates by inductive abstraction from similar beings something universal, namely not an ape, but a human being, which exists in him really, although only potentially. Aristotle writes: "Thus it is clear that it is necessary for us to become familiar with the primitives by induction; for perception too instils the universal in this way."[45] If the universal is abstracted, it exists potentially in the individual, but actually only in the human mind.

This brings Aristotle close to conceptualism. However, for conceptualism, contrary to the realism of Plato or Aristotle, the universals are not real, but exist only in thoughts or representations. Locke writes in *An Essay Concerning Human Understanding*:

---

42 Cat., Chapter 5, 2a12-14. Transl. Ackrill.

43 Metaph., Book 7, Chapter 13, 1038b8-9. Transl. Ross.

44 Expression taken from Donald Cary Williams (1899-1983), cf. my article, Metaphysische Perle.

45 Analytica posteriora, Chapter 19, 100b4-5. Transl. Barnes.

> To conclude: this whole *mystery* of *genera* and *species*, which make such a noise in the schools, and are with justice so little regarded out of them, is nothing else but abstract *ideas*, more or less comprehensive, with names annexed to them. In all which, this is constant and unvariable: that every more general term stands for such an *idea* as is but a part of any of those contained under it.[46]

To give an example: The name "human being" stands for the idea of a human being and contains only part of what we mean by that concept. But while for Plato the term "*eidos*", or "*idea*", means something objective that exists independently of human beings, for Locke it means something subjective that is created by human beings. In contrast to Aristotle's view, however, for Locke, universals do not really exist in the particular.

We can sum up the comparison by means of a medieval characterisation: For Platonic realism, the universals exist "before the things" *(ante rem)*; for Aristotelian realism, they exist "in the things" *(in re)*; and for conceptualism, they exist only "after the things" *(post rem)*.

Yet, according to my above assumption, classes do not have a real, but only a semantic, existence (cf. p. 109). Genera and species, as classes, likewise have no real existence, but only a semantic existence. We obviously do not see the meaning of words with our bodily eyes. Thus, nobody has ever seen the meaning of the universal terms "human being" or "living being" with their bodily eyes, either as something separate from, or as something real within, the world of the senses.

The existence of an intellectual intuition of these universals is too uncertain to provide a firm starting point to prove the real and mind-independent existence of genera and species (cf. pp. 107-108). Only a disembodied soul could perhaps be taken to be capable of seeing not only particular things, but also something universal without a universal name, that is, without a linguistic symbol. But the existence of a soul without a body is even less certain than that of an intellectual intuition without linguistic symbols. Even if there is such a thing as an intellectual intuition of extramental universals, and even if universals exist as independent entities, there still remains the open question of how we are to imagine the relationship between these universals and the sensory phenomena.

Plato uses a diverse selection of images, such as the participation of sensory phenomena in the ideas, or the copy of ideas in the sensory phenomena, to illustrate this relation. The metaphor of participation, as used by Plato,

46 Locke, Essay Concerning Human Understanding, Book 3, Chapter 3, section 9.

suggests that the ideas exist beyond and apart from the sensory phenomena, while the metaphor of copy suggests that they are contained within them. But if the transcendent ideas are within the sensory phenomena, then "the *one* man, the *one* ox, the *one* beautiful and the *one* good"[47] is either "dispersed and *multiplied* in the infinity of the world of generation" or exists "as still entire and yet divided from itself". "The latter of which", writes Plato, "would seem to be the greatest impossibility of all, for how can one and the same thing be at the same time in one and in many things?"[48] Thus, the relationship between ideas and sensory phenomena leads us into a contradiction. Plato's possibly last word on the matter in the *Timaeus* is that sensory phenomena are "the imitations of real existences [that is, ideas] modelled after their pattern in a wonderful way which is hard to explain and which we will subsequently investigate".[49] Unfortunately, he does not seem to have investigated this question later as explicitly as one might wish.

In contrast, Aristotle's position is closer to our own understanding of reality in that it recognises that universals have no separate existence, but depend on particulars. The relationship between sensory phenomena and ideas which was "hard to explain" for Plato now turns into the everyday predication of a universal based on a particular. This enables Aristotle to avoid the Platonic separation of universals from particulars, since the universals exist in the particulars of which they are predicated. However, Aristotle, too, assumes an intellectual intuition as the precondition for perceiving the universal. Aristotle's position, then, also leads to a contradiction.

His position is, in fact, the mirror image of Plato's. If the universal exists in the particulars, it is either individualised or a particular, and can no longer be grasped by a universal name. The quality of being human appears in Socrates, Plato, Aristotle, et al., in their individual form. Yet, this raises the question of how an individualised universal can still be universal, that is, common to different individuals, such as Socrates, Plato, Aristotle, etc., and occur in different places and times. Aristotle seems to solve this problem by arguing that universals are only potentially in particulars and are only universal due to our capacity for intellectual abstraction. But in so doing, he falls victim to a crucial problem of conceptualism.

According to conceptualism, genera and species exist only as thoughts or concepts in the human mind. This would make them ideas or representa-

47 Phlb. 15 a. My translation and emphasis.
48 Phlb. 15 b. My translation and emphasis.
49 Ti. 50 c. My translation. Cf. my paper Theory of Ideas in *Timaeus.*

tions. However, ideas or representations are parts of a particular soul and, therefore, no longer universal but rather individual and subjective (cf. p. 35). And, to quote Frege, if universals are subjective, they are no longer the "shared property of many people".[50] Furthermore, according to the law of existential generalisation, if we regard the proposition "The human being is a living being" as true, then we assume that the class of human beings exists (cf. p. 95). This implies not only that our representation of the class exists, but that the extra-mental class of human beings itself exists.

In saying "The human being is a living being", we also not only say that the linguistic utterance "the human being" in the sense of a verbal entity does exist. When we put forward such true propositions, we are thinking not only of something that lies outside our mind, but also of something that exists outside our linguistic utterances, that is, the extra-mental and extra-linguistic class of human beings. When uttering the proposition "The human being is a living being", we do not mean that the general name of the class of human beings exists, but rather that the class of human beings itself exists. But if general names like "human being" that refer to the many individual humans have meaning, they cannot be mere verbal entities or *flatus vocis*, that is, "breath of our voice" without signification, as the radical claim of nominalism would have it.

Thus, neither realism nor conceptualism nor extreme nominalism can satisfactorily answer Porphyry's question about how genera and species exist. Realism claims too much, while conceptualism and, above all, extreme nominalism claim too little.

If genera and species have only semantic existences, then universals exist neither as realities nor as thoughts nor as nouns, but only as the meanings of nouns. In contrast to *Platonic* or *real* Platonism, I will call this view *Semantic* Platonism. According to this view, universals exist, as in real Platonism: While universals are "invisible and imperceptible by any sense",[51] they nevertheless exist, but in a different way from sensory phenomena. In contrast to the view in real Platonism, however, universals are not "ungenerated and indestructible",[52] but rather are created by human beings. Only human beings can give the universal nouns a meaning, which they then turn into the referent.

In saying this, I am applying Frege's remark ("The indirect reference of a word is accordingly its customary sense") not only to propositions (cf. p.

50 Frege, Sinn and Bedeutung, p. 146. Transl. Geach and Black, Beaney, p. 154.
51 Ti. 52 a.
52 Ti. 52 a.

110), but also to universals. We could call this the reification of the meaning of abstract nouns. If semantic objects of this kind exist, universals, unlike sensory phenomena, have no kind of existence that can be experienced through the senses, but rather only semantic existence. Universals do not exist objectively, in the strong sense of being independent from human beings, but only in the weak sense in which we take their intersubjective identity for granted.

Like Aristotle, Semantic Platonism assumes that we often obtain the same intersubjective meaning by abstracting out the similarities between individuals. This is most noticeable in the case of natural species, which also include human beings, at least to some extent. Thus, we obtain the universal name "human being" in distinction to "ape" by abstraction from the perceptible properties shared by the many different individual humans.

Like conceptualism, Semantic Platonism assumes that universals are human creations. Thus, it is a labour of intellectual abstraction that creates the shared meaning of the name "human being", which we then make the object of our speech.

Like nominalism, Semantic Platonism assumes that, in reality, only the particular exists, and the universal resides in universal nouns. Yet, I must stress once more that, in opposition to extreme nominalism, the universal here does not exist in universal nouns as strings of sounds or letters (which vary from one human being to another), but rather in the meanings of these nouns.

Semantic Platonism, then, tries to integrate elements of Platonism, Aristotelianism, conceptualism and nominalism, without postulating the reality of universals or denying their intersubjective sameness.

If the meanings of universal nouns are made the referents, it may appear as if they are perceived directly or "seen". However, what we see, for example, in the proposition "Human beings are living beings" is not a physical human being, but only something like or a scheme of a human being or a quasi-human. Therefore, Semantic Platonism, too, is only something like Platonism – a "Quasi-Platonism" – and the vision of the universals is only something like a vision – or "quasi-vision".

Yet, "Quasi-Platonism" also gives real Platonism "the place which is its due"[53] if we regard it at least as a heuristic device to search further, for example, in mathematics for the discovery of abstract entities and in philosophy for *the* Good.

---

53 Frege, Thought, 342. My translation.

Admittedly, Semantic Platonism is, like Platonic or real Platonism, "difficult to accept", but also difficult "not to accept".[54] It is "difficult to accept" because we have no clear-cut criterion for the identity of such airy constructs as semantic objects, although we presuppose their identity. This was stressed in particular by Quine.[55] We can see, for example, that an individual is the same today as yesterday and, if necessary, we are able to verify that individual's identity by comparing fingerprints. But how can we tell that the invisible meaning of the universal name "human being" that we used yesterday is not something different today? We must probably be content, in the spirit of Wittgenstein, with the fact of a successful communication over time *within* a language community, when we say, for example, "The human being is a living being".

In yet another respect, Semantic Platonism is "difficult not to accept" because we rely on universal semantic objects and their identity not only in the sciences, but also in our everyday communication. Aristotle aptly formulated this idea as follows: "Not to have one definite meaning is to have no meaning, and if words have no meaning our talking with one another, and indeed with ourselves, has been annihilated."[56]

b) The Being of Fictitious Things and the Being of Nothingness

The concept of semantic existence allows me to address a further problem, namely, the problem of the being of fictitious things – for example, golden mountains, winged horses, talking cows, centaurs, etc. – as well as the problem of the being of nothingness. Fictitious things, unlike a real mountain, a real horse, a real cow or a real human being, are things that have no real existence. But fictitious things, unlike logically impossible things (such as a round square), are logically possible. Therefore, facts that include fictitious things do not necessarily contravene the law of non-contradiction. It is no logical contradiction to say that a horse can have wings or that a cow can speak, even though in reality there are no horses with wings or talking cows. However, a square cannot be round for logical reasons. For a round square is not a square.

---

54 R. 532 d. My translation.

55 Cf. e.g. Word and Object, § 43, pp. 200-206.

56 Metaph., Book 4, Chapter 4, 1006b7-11. Transl. Ross with modifications. Cf. Prm. 135b-c.

What, then, is the ontological status of things that are not? Fictitious things and nothingness do not exist. If we say (a) "There is no golden mountain" or (b) "There is no nothingness", we are putting forward a true proposition. But the prerequisite of a true proposition is that there is *something about which* it says something is true. Therefore, from the true proposition (a) follows the true proposition (a'): "There *is* an x, for which it is the case that *this x* is a golden mountain." Likewise, from the true proposition (b) follows the true proposition (b'): "There *is* an x, for which it is the case that *this x* is nothingness." From the negation of the existence of fictitious things and of nothingness follows the affirmation of their existence. But the negation *and* affirmation of the existence of fictitious things and nothingness leads to a contradiction. Thus, the ontological status of things that are not appears contradictory, in that they do not exist and yet they exist nonetheless.
This contradiction disappears if we make a distinction between real and semantic existence. The corollaries of propositions (a) and (b) are propositions (a') and (b'). But in (a) and (b), it is not stated whether a golden mountain and nothingness have real or semantic existence. Nobody has ever seen a mountain in nature made entirely out of gold. Likewise, nobody has ever literally seen nothingness (even though many have faced nothingness in a figurative sense). Therefore, golden mountains and nothingness do not really exist, but only semantically exist, insofar as we can talk about golden mountains and nothingness meaningfully, that is, without a logical contradiction. Martin Heidegger thought that he could make meaningful statements even about nothingness, for example: "*Das Nichts nichtet*" – "The nothing nothings."[57]
Propositions (a) and (b) must, then, be rephrased as (α) "There is no real golden mountain" and (β) "There is no real nothingness", and (a') and (b') as (α') "There is a semantic x, which means that this x is a golden mountain" and (β') "There is a semantic x, which means that this x is nothingness". The two propositions, (α) "There is no real golden mountain" and (α') "There is a semantic golden mountain", contradict each other as little as the propositions (β) "There is no real nothingness" and (β') "There is a semantic nothingness".
Such negative existential propositions, therefore, deny the existence of a real referent in expressions such as "a golden mountain" and "nothingness", but do not deny the meaning or the semantic referent. Here, rather, the

---

57 Metaphysics, Section 3, 31. Transl. Quine, Quiddities, p. 240 (instead of Krell's translation).

meaning of the expression itself becomes the referent. Therefore, I can once again apply Frege's remark ("The indirect reference of a word is accordingly its customary sense")[58] to fictitious objects, where the referent is not an object in the external world but the meaning of an expression (as in the case of the golden mountains). While representations are private, even though with the expression "golden mountain" we refer to something shared, the meaning of "golden mountain" cannot be located in our world of representation. Moreover, when we speak of a golden mountain, we do not mean our representation of a golden mountain, but an extramental golden mountain. However, when the sense or meaning of the expression becomes the referent, *the meaning itself* has an existence (albeit a merely semantic one). We may refer to this process as the reification of the meaning of names for fictitious things.

It is for this very reason that the law of existential generalisation (cf. p. 95) does not apply in an unqualified sense to negative existential propositions. It is actually necessary to indicate the context in which it does apply, whether in the real or in the semantic world. Where negative existential propositions about fictitious objects are concerned, we must modify the law of existential generalisation to ensure that the existential propositions concerned deny only real, but not semantic, existence. Thus, the proposition "There is no golden mountain" denies the *real* existence of a golden mountain, but not its semantic existence. Indeed, in order to be true, it tacitly assumes its semantic existence. Since negative existential propositions about fictitious objects do not deny but rather tacitly assume their semantic existence, what follows from a negative existential proposition about fictitious objects is not their real existence, but rather their semantic existence.

This is how the distinction between real and semantic existence can solve the problem of how we are able to talk meaningfully about things that do not exist. A fictitious thing, like an abstract thing, has no real existence, but only a semantic existence.

On another note, we must also observe that logically impossible things like round squares do not even have semantic existence. The expression "round square" does not express anything definite and has insofar no meaning (cf. pp. 111-112). Thus, the proposition "There is no round square" denies not only the real existence, but also the semantic existence of a round square. In order to be true, it assumes only the verbal existence of a round square,

58 Frege, Sinn and Bedeutung, p. 145. Transl. Geach and Black with modification, Beaney, p. 154.

that is, the existence of the meaningless combination of the two linguistic expressions "round" and "square" which has no semantic referent. Here again Aristotle's remark applies: "Not to have one definite meaning is to have no meaning, and if words have no meaning our talking with one another, and indeed with ourselves, has been annihilated."[59]

What has been claimed above does not, however, entail that I need not recognise a difference between abstract and fictitious objects. While the former seems indispensable to the sciences, for example, mathematics, physics and biology, the latter (say, the gods of Homer) are creations that are accepted only within a particular framework (in this case, of ancient mythology). Golden mountains may exist only in the fairy-tale world of the Grimm brothers, and Polonius and Ophelia only in Shakespeare's *Hamlet*. In contrast to what really exists, what exists semantically is created by human beings.

In addition, this sort of existence is context-dependent, since it only makes sense within a framework of existential settings – whether that framework be Cantor's set theory, modern physics and biology, Greek mythology, Grimm's fairy tales, or Shakespeare's *Hamlet*. The essential difference between abstract objects and fictitious ones is that the contexts in which they exist are different. But, however disparate numbers, ideal mass points, natural species, Homer's gods, golden mountains, and Polonius and Ophelia may be, so far as function and content are concerned, they all have only semantic existence.

There is also, of course, a sense in which real existence is itself context-dependent. While real existence depends on the context of the specific experience of human beings, it does not, however, depend on any of the contexts I have mentioned within that experience. Once we have made this distinction between the context of the experience of the human species and the specific context within that experience, we can simplify matters by saying that real existence is context-*independent*, while semantic existence is context-*dependent*.

Thus, our explanation of the concept of "being" answers the question "What exists, or what facts are the case?" in stating that both real and semantic facts are the case. Since real facts can be either physical or psychic in nature, we can also say that physical, psychic and semantic facts are the case. Such a distinction between three kinds of fact can be called (to use

59 Metaph., Book 4, Chapter 4, 1006b7-11. Transl. Ross with modifications. Cf. Prm. 135b-c.

Popper's phrase) an ontology of three worlds.[60] The physical world is the totality of all physical facts, the psychic world is the totality of all psychic facts and the semantic world is the totality of all semantic facts.

However, a more fundamental distinction is the distinction between not three, but two worlds, that is, the real and the semantic. It goes without saying that the concept of being, which we assumed to be a precondition for this explanatory distinction, does not belong to the real world. For the concept of being, there is no experience, either internal or external. As Kant says, "Being is obviously not a real predicate".[61] But neither is nothingness a real predicate. The concept of nothingness – insofar as we can talk meaningfully about it – like that of being, belongs in the semantic world.

---

60 Popper, Objective Knowledge, Chapter 4, pp. 158-197, esp. Section 4, pp. 164-167.

61 Kant, CPR, A 599/B 624. Transl. Guyer and Wood.

VI. Good

1. *The Good, Morally and Extramorally*

Among all of the things that exist, some stand out in our eyes by being good. But what is *the* good? According to the classic definition, which goes back to Plato and Aristotle, the good is "that at which all things aim".[1] If all things aim at the good, all human beings do so as well. Therefore, we can adapt the classic definition as follows: The good is that at which every human being aims.

This definition is, however, confronted by a further, yet still-open, question, namely, "Is what *every* human being aims at the good?" We must answer this question in the negative. It is not the case that what everybody aims at is always the good. Everyone seems to aim at pleasure, for example, but does that make pleasure the good? We cannot answer this question in the affirmative, because there are obviously bad pleasures, for example, the pleasures of the sadist. Thus, the concept of the good, too, contains a surplus meaning, which is not rendered by the classic definition. What I have said about the concept of truth and the concept of being also applies to the concept of the good: It cannot be defined explicitly, but only implicitly. To put it differently: It can only be elucidated. To elucidate the concept of the good is to make conscious what we already know about it in an undeveloped, that is, unclear and indistinct form.

In elucidating this concept of the good, it is once again advisable to begin with language. Like the terms "true" and "is", the noun "the good" has *several* meanings, between which the classic definition – "that at which all things aim" – makes no distinction. In accordance with the noun "the good", the adjective "good" also has several meanings. When we say "A glass of wine is good", we do not mean the same thing as when we say "A will or an intention is good". In the first instance, we mean that a glass of wine is a good means to an end, say, our health or enjoyment. In the second instance, we mean that a will or an intention is good in itself. In the first instance, we invest the term "good" with a relative or instrumental meaning. In the second instance, we invest it with a (comparatively) abso-

1 Aristotle, EN, Book 1, Chapter 1, 1094a2-3. Transl. Ross. Cf. Plato, Grg. 468 b, 499c-500 a, R. 505d-e and my article *Ho de diôkei*.

lute or moral meaning. In what follows, I do not discuss what is good merely in an instrumental or relative sense, but rather what is good in itself or is good in a moral sense. The discipline that examines the good in such ways is called ethics.

According to an apt definition by G. E. Moore (1873-1958) in his *Principia Ethica*, ethics is "the general enquiry into what is good".[2] However, since we have confined ourselves to the morally good, I can narrow the definition down for our purposes as follows: Ethics is the general inquiry into what is morally good. By morality, I mean the kind of practical behaviour that corresponds to the theory of ethics.

What is morally good can be felt or spoken about. When we speak about what is good, we express ourselves in sentences that are not only descriptive but also evaluative. We judge human beings and their qualities, among other things, as good or bad, and judge their actions as right or wrong. Ethics, then, examines not only what is good and right, but also what is bad and wrong. What is good should be done, and what is bad should be avoided. What is neither good and right nor bad and wrong, but is merely indifferent, may be either done or avoided. This is why the language of morality comprises not only evaluative sentences, but also sentences that command, forbid or permit something. In the language of morality, those sentences that either command or forbid something are particularly significant. They are also called normative sentences.

Now, since values and norms are two different things, evaluative sentences are not normative sentences. The value of human life, for example, is not the same as the norm proscribing the destruction of human life. The value of human life, is, rather, the foundation of this norm, which we feel in our conscience. (Conscience may be considered the awareness of the normative claim of values.) In a similar way, the normative sentence "Though shalt not kill" – or again more precisely its content, *the proposition* which the sentence expresses – is grounded in the evaluative proposition "Human life is valuable".

An examination of these evaluative and normative propositions is not, in itself, an evaluative or normative ethic. It does not tell us what is good or bad, right or wrong, to be done or not to be done. It only talks *about* the propositions we use to say that something is good or bad or right or wrong, or that we should do this and not that. This is why this kind of examination is also called *meta*ethics. Metaethics is the study of moral language, and it includes, in particular, two theories of evaluative or norma-

---

2 Moore, PE, Chapter 1, § 2, p. 2.

tive propositions or statements, the first being called cognitivism and the second emotivism.

2. The Metaethics of Moral Good

a) Cognitivism

The most obvious metaethical theory is cognitivism. According to this theory, moral propositions have the same status as those statements we use to express an insight. It seems clear that we can just as easily tell what is good or bad – right or wrong – as we can tell what is black and what is white. In both instances, we only need to open our eyes. That it is morally right to dress a bleeding wound, and morally wrong to let a person bleed to death, seems to be as clearly visible as the fact that snow is white and pitch is black.

This theory has several advantages. First, it agrees with our evaluative moral language. We speak in the indicative about moral properties ("X is good or bad, right or wrong"), as well as about natural ones ("X is white or black"), and we attribute the values true and false to moral propositions as well as to assertions of facts. Furthermore, this theory can easily explain the absolute validity that we attribute to *certain* moral values by stressing their reality and objectivity. Moreover, this kind of thinking we call *realism* in ethics and epistemology is a basic attitude of common sense and a recurrent philosophy. It has been advocated by the majority of philosophers from Plato and Aristotle to G. E. Moore and others.[3] Finally, realism has the advantage that, unlike ethical scepticism (which claims that we can never recognise anything as indisputably good or bad), it is not so readily abandoned outside philosophy.

A particularly strong formulation of ethical realism is found in *Memoirs from the House of the Dead* by Fyodor Mikhailovich Dostoevsky (1821-1881):

> There are certain crimes which, from the beginning of the world, under every code of law, have always and everywhere been regarded as indisputably crimes and will continue to be so regarded while men are men.

---

3 Cf. e.g. Plato, R., Book 4, 427d-434 c; Book 6, 504a-506 a; Book 7, 534b-c. Aristotle, EN, Book I, Chapter 1, 1094 a 22-26. Moore, PE, Chapter 1, § 10, pp. 9-10.

Among such crimes would be the murder of a whole people, or genocide, for example. Conversely, we can say that some deeds are undeniably morally right and will remain so as long as human beings remain human beings. It is, for example, undeniably right for one human being or one nation to save another from starvation.

Cognitivism, then, leads to moral objectivism and realism. It recognises moral facts in reality. These facts are objective insofar as they exist in themselves and not just for us, the fact that genocide is bad and saving people from starvation is good being examples of such. The fundamental thesis of cognitivism can be formulated as follows: Moral sentences (or, more accurately, their content, the propositions) are true or false because they either correspond or do not correspond with moral facts.

Among these moral facts, we can distinguish two kinds: the basic and the derived. A basic or indeed "axiomatic" moral fact is conveyed by the first statement of the Constitution of the Federal Republic of Germany: "Human dignity is inviolable." From this "axiomatic" proposition, it is possible to "derive" others, such as that every human being has the right to life and physical integrity, and that the freedom of the individual is uninfringeable (Article 2.1).

But how do we come to recognise moral facts? Obviously, moral facts cannot be real facts of a physical nature, such as the fact that snow is white and pitch is black. Although even such physical facts are really hypothetical, moral qualities are downright invisible. We can see with our own eyes the white colour of snow and the black colour of pitch, but we cannot read the moral quality of a face or an action directly from the outside. A face may seem friendly to us and yet its smile may hide unfriendly thoughts. The features of a criminal, as a rule, are no different from those of "decent" people – as any visitor to a prison can confirm. An action like the transfer of a bleeding person from one car to another may be a rescue or a kidnapping.

The qualities "good", "bad", "right" or "wrong" have no effect on our sensory organs, or at least not the same effect as the qualities "white" or "black". Likewise, just by looking at Mr Smith or Mrs Jones, we cannot immediately tell that they possess inviolable dignity. Since we do not perceive these moral qualities with our bodily eyes, cognitivism was able to conceive of the idea that such moral qualities are of a "supernatural" or metaphysical nature and can only be "seen" with a "mind's eye". We do not see with our bodily eye that it is right to dress a bleeding wound, but wrong to let a person bleed to death, or that a human being possesses inviolable dignity. In order to "see" such things we must "open our intellectual eye".

The hypothesis of direct intellectual vision is by no means restricted to "seeing" mathematical or geometrical axioms, such as "The whole is greater than the part" (cf. p. 61). Rather, it has been transferred from "seeing" mathematical and geometrical axioms to "seeing" moral ones. Since we also cannot see moral facts, even though they somehow seem to exist, the linguistic expedient of talking about non-sensory vision seemed appropriate. Cognitivism thus leads to *intuitionism* (a term based upon the Latin *intueor*, meaning "I gaze").

Yet, it was precisely this intellectual intuition itself that facilitated a decisive argument against objectivism, namely, that intuition as an objective criterion is no more true of moral axioms than it is of the axioms of arithmetic and geometry. The intuitively plausible axiom that the whole is greater than the part, for example, is not true for infinite quantities (cf. p. 62). Likewise, even an eye as sharp as that of Aristotle failed to "see" the inviolable dignity of the human being and the uninfringeable freedom of the individual, believing, as he did, that some people were slaves by nature (cf. p. 78). It takes an intuition that has grown and developed historically, that is, an acquired intuition, to "see" such an axiom in its universal binding force.

Yet, even such an acquired intuition may come up against borderline cases in which it no longer sees clearly. Does a person who has been in a coma for the past seventeen years still have inviolable dignity? Moral intuition, like mathematical intuition, may offer prima facie evidence (cf. p. 63), but it by no means guarantees the impartiality claimed by the objectivist. It can be corrected or even abrogated by other "intuitions", as it is, for example, in the case of passive or, occasionally even active, euthanasia.

The objectivity of such intuition is also not alone open to doubt. There is also a possible argument against the concept of moral facts. Moral facts are not only facts but also norms. The dignity of the human being inviolable is a fact as well as a norm. The very *fact* of the dignity of the human being inviolable amounts to *a ban on* violating human dignity. If human dignity *is* inviolable, it follows that it *ought* not be violated (i.e. its violation is forbidden). If killing *is* morally wrong, then thou *shalt* not kill (i.e. killing is forbidden). If moral judgments are statements of facts, a constative proposition gives rise to a normative one.

Here, it may be objected that it is inadmissible to infer a normative proposition from a constative one. Since this objection goes back to Hume's *Treatise of Human Nature*, it is also called "Hume's Law" and states that one cannot derive an "ought" from an "is".[4] In any valid deductive conclusion, the content must not go beyond that of the premises. A valid deductive conclusion is truth-preserving (cf. p. 45). However, if a normative conclusion is inferred from constative premises, the conclusion does not preserve the truth of the premises but rather goes beyond their meaning. It adds something new, which was not contained in the premises, namely, an obligation.

Cognitivism and intuitionism regard evaluative and normative sentences such as "Killing is wrong" or "Thou shalt not kill" – or more precisely its content, *the proposition* which the sentences express – as constative statements in linguistic disguise. As such, such propositions are true or false insofar as they correspond or do not correspond with moral facts. Yet, according to "Hume's Law", it is not possible to derive normative propositions from them. If the proposition "Killing is wrong" or "Thou shalt not kill" state a fact, then "thou shalt" does not have normative, but only constative, force. In this case, however, the ban on killing is not itself a ban, but merely a statement of the ban, and it seems that no valid norm can be derived from it. Like the derivation of an "ought" from an "is", on the basis of "Hume's Law", it thus seems "altogether inconceivable"[5] how moral facts could exist. While a moral fact would necessarily imply a norm, it is "altogether inconceivable" how a mere fact could imply a norm. This obliterates the decisive reason for any moral realism, objectivism and cognitivism: Where there are no moral facts in reality, there are no objective moral facts either. Where there are no objective moral facts, there is nothing that can be objectively recognised.

b) Emotivism

As an alternative to cognitivism, we are offered Hume's hypothesis that moral propositions such as "X is good or bad / right or wrong" have no cognitive content and only serve to describe our feelings. If, for example, I say that premeditated murder is wrong, this proposition renders neither a natural fact about the empirical world nor a metaphysical fact about an invisible world, but merely describes my internal experience. It describes a sense of revulsion or outrage that I feel in the face of premeditated murder. Our moral language, then, constantly leads us into deception. It pretends

4 Hume, Treatise, Book 3, Part 1, Section 1, pp. 469-470.
5 Ibid. p. 469.

to describe real properties when, in fact, only our emotions are real. This is why this position is called emotivism. Since these feelings are described by moral propositions, we can also call this form of emotivism descriptive emotivism. And, because emotions are normally regarded as subjective, we can also talk about a *descriptive moral subjectivism*.

Yet, here we can even go a step further. A proposition such as "X is good or right, bad or wrong", despite its descriptive *form*, need not have a descriptive *function*. As we have seen, there is no necessary connection between the form of a sentence and its function (cf. p. 31). A moral proposition such as "X is good or right / bad or wrong" need not be a description, despite its descriptive form, but may also have an *expressive* purpose. According to this position, a proposition such as "Killing is wrong" is neither true nor false, because it can neither correspond nor not correspond with an internal or external fact. Rather, it has the same function as pronouncing "killing" in a particularly indignant tone.[6] This type of emotivism we can also call *expressive moral emotivism* or *expressive moral subjectivism*. In contrast to descriptive emotivism or subjectivism, in the theory of expressive emotivism, moral propositions do not represent moral facts at all (not even internal facts). Moral propositions only express feelings. In so doing, such propositions can also "arouse feelings" in other people and "stimulate action".[7]

There is, however, a counter-argument against both kinds of emotivism or subjectivism: We can obviously pass contradictory moral judgments and disagree, with good reasons, about moral propositions as well as about assertions of facts. For example, in a debate about whether or not abortion is reprehensible, a strong case can be made for either view. If moral judgments were only descriptions or expressions of feelings, they could not be contradictory, and there would be no point in looking for reasons to argue

---

6 This view is held, for example, by Alfred Ayer (1910-1989), Language, Truth and Logic, Chapter 6, p. 107: "If now I generalise my previous statement and say, 'Stealing money is wrong,' I produce a sentence which has no factual meaning – that is, expresses no proposition which can be either true or false. It is as if I had written 'Stealing money!!' – where the shape and thickness of the exclamation marks show, by a suitable convention, that a special sort of moral disapproval is the feeling which is being expressed. It is clear that there is nothing said here which can be true or false."

7 Cf. Ayer, Language, Truth and Logic: "It is worth mentioning that ethical terms do not serve only to express feeling. They are calculated also to arouse feeling, and so to stimulate action. ... In fact we may define the meaning of the various ethical words in terms both of the different feelings they are ordinarily taken to express, and also the different responses which they are calculated to provoke." p. 109.

about whether or not they are right. Feelings can conflict. A man can love and hate a woman at one and the same time, and a woman can likewise love and hate a man. But in a logical sense, feelings cannot contradict themselves, as propositions can.

With regard to morally indifferent things, for example, smoking in the street, the constative form of a sentence such as "Smoking is wrong" need not necessarily have a morally relevant content. Coming from an *ordinary* non-smoker, it may function as a simple personal expression, but if it is said by a *fanatical* non-smoker, it represents for him a moral fact. It also matters, then, *who* makes the statement in question.

Yet, to give another example, if a morally relevant basic proposition such as "Genocide is morally wrong" merely expresses feelings, the opposite, "Genocide is morally right", would do the same. Since both are only expressions of emotions in disguise, there would be no point in arguing, with reasons, about which is right and which is wrong.

In addition, when it comes to moral basic propositions of the kind I have mentioned, the emotivist conception runs counter not only to our theoretical basic convictions, which we express in descriptive and objectivist language, but also to the demand for generalisation that we attach to such moral basic propositions. If we describe an action as morally wrong, we are expressing an attitude that we expect others to share. "Murder is morally wrong" means not only that "murder is morally wrong for me", but also that "murder is morally wrong for anybody". Conversely, it would seem unacceptable to us if somebody said, "It is wrong if I secretly kill my rich aunt, but it is not wrong for me, because I will profit from her death". If it is wrong to kill my rich aunt, then it is also wrong for me.

This demand for generalisation is shown particularly clearly by the fact that moral basic propositions are socially sanctioned. If I do not observe them, I have to face a diversity of negative social sanctions, such as prison, a fine, withdrawal of social respect and other punishments. If moral basic propositions were only of a personal nature, it would be difficult to see why other people should be able to punish me for disregarding them. On the other hand, a mere expression – such as "Murder, how horrible" – is no more capable of socially sanctioned generalisation than an account of my personal feelings. Given the same facts, both the expressions and the accounts of our feelings can turn out very differently. I cannot expect other people to share my feelings. Nor can I expect my deviating expressions and emotions to be binding for other people. In addition, other people do not have the right to punish me for my deviant feelings, or for my deviant moral expressions and emotions.

Emotivism, whether expressive or descriptive, can hardly justify the socially sanctioned demand for the generalisation of moral basic propositions, which distinguishes such basic propositions from mere exclamations and personal accounts of feelings. Nevertheless, expressive emotivism has the merit of drawing attention to the non-cognitive, expressive and action-guiding function that distinguishes moral basic propositions from merely descriptive ones. Moral basic propositions also serve to voice either commendation or condemnation, from which it is possible to derive norms as to what should be done and what should be avoided.

This gives rise to two demands that a satisfactory metaethical theory can be expected to fulfil: (a) a metaethical theory must take account of the cognitive and objective element in moral basic propositions and of the descriptive language of morality, and (b) it must at the same time do justice to the emotive and subjective element (made up of commendation and condemnation) in moral basic propositions, so that normative propositions can be derived from those descriptive ones.

But the two demands seem to lead to a contradiction and to be incompatible. If moral basic propositions are cognitive and contain an objective and descriptive element, they can be generalised. But then no norms can be derived from them. If moral basic propositions are emotive and contain a subjective and non-descriptive element, it is possible to derive norms from them. Yet, in such a case, are the moral basic propositions still descriptive and able to be generalised?

c) Institutionalism

To resolve this contradiction, we may regard basic moral propositions, such as "It is right to dress a bleeding wound, but wrong to let a person bleed to death", as descriptions of *institutional* facts. Basic moral facts, then, do not exist in themselves, either in the physical world or in an invisible metaphysical world, as cognitivism suggests, nor are they merely subjective psychic facts, as descriptive emotivism assumes. But neither are they non-existent.

Basic moral facts exist, but they are of an institutional nature. Accordingly, morality is neither something objective nor something subjective. It is, rather, something essentially social, that is, an institution made by human beings. In so far as a moral institution, such as the ban on killing, exists regardless of whether or not I recognise it, such a moral institution is not subjective, but objective. However, in so far as it is constituted by a language community, it is not objective in the strong sense of existing independently of a language community. It is objective only in an intersubjective sense. It is valid among different people and, in the case of moral basic propositions, among all people, precisely because it is supposed to set standards for all. (To avoid losing our way in a debate on exceptions, I will deal only with moral basic positions, such as the ban on killing in general, and ignore exceptions such as self-defence, killing in war, capital punishment, suicide, and passive or active euthanasia.)

The term "institutional fact" was introduced by Searle in his book *Speech Acts.*[8] Institutional facts are objective and not just a matter of feeling. Nevertheless, they cannot be reduced to real facts. Examples of such institutional facts given by Searle are as follows:

> Mr Smith married Miss Jones; the Dodgers beat the Giants three to two in eleven innings; Green was convicted of larceny; and Congress passed the Appropriation Bill.[9]

Unlike a real, that is, merely physical or psychic fact, an institutional fact comes into being as a result of constitutive rules. These rules are structured as follows: "X stands for Y in the context of community C." They are called constitutive because they constitute X as Y. But since they constitute X as Y in the context of the language community LC, they are also semantic rules. These rules give X a certain meaning Y in the context of a language community LC. A real physical action X in the context of a language community LC is given the meaning Y, which may, for example, be a marriage, a victory, a theft or a ratification.

Institutional facts, then, are real facts, interpreted in a specific way. In institutional facts, the real world and the semantic world enter a certain association. This association, with regard to institutional facts, is of a normative nature. Therefore, Miss Jones, by marrying Mr Smith, accepts some obligations towards Mr Smith, as does Mr Smith towards Miss Jones by marrying her.

If we enter for Y a normative or evaluative concept – that is, the meaning of a normative or evaluative expression – such institutional facts can also contain norms or values. Among such institutional facts of a moral nature, I count the basic moral facts, such as the fact that it is morally right to dress a bleeding wound, but wrong to let a person bleed to death, or that genocide is morally wrong, but preventing death by starvation is morally

---

8 Searle, Speech Acts, Chapter 2, Section 7, pp. 50-53.

9 Searle, ibid. p. 51.

right.[10] A certain physical action (or omission) X – such as dressing a wound or allowing a person to bleed to death, genocide or supplying food, for example – is turned by constitutive rules into Y, that is, into an action that is morally right or wrong. Since the physical action X represents a physical fact, we can say that physical facts are turned into institutional facts by constitutive rules.

But psychic facts, for example, Mr Smith's jealousy over Miss Jones or Miss Jones' jealousy over Mr Smith, can also turn into institutional facts. Jealousy is generally attributed a negative value, being regarded as a "vice". Therefore, it is possible to derive from it the norm of not being jealous. Conversely, the lack of jealousy is generally attributed a positive value and regarded as a "virtue", so that it is possible to derive from it the norm, to have a big heart. But since "virtues" and "vices" represent inner attitudes and are not immediately visible from outside, the social sanctions are also less obvious. A so-called inchoate offence, such as the desire of Mr Smith to kill Miss Jones or the desire of Miss Jones to kill Mr. Smith, does not produce sanctions until it is somehow articulated or until preparations for the action become known. Likewise, jealousy and magnanimity, envy and lack of envy, etc., are not assigned either a negative or a positive value until they become visible. But *then* internal facts or facts of consciousness also provoke external reactions from other people.

Semantic facts, too, can turn into institutional facts. By ignoring an individual murder and formulating the abstract proposition "Murder is morally wrong", we turn a semantic fact into an institutional one. We then no longer refer to an individual murder, but to the meaning of the statement "Murder is morally wrong". Therefore, not an individual murder but the meaning of the proposition "Murder is morally wrong" itself becomes the referent. Likewise, the first article of the German constitution "Human dignity is inviolable" is an institutional fact of a semantic nature. This statement does not refer to the inviolable dignity of Mr Smith or Miss Jones, but to the inviolable dignity of the human being in an abstract sense. From this institutional fact it is possible to derive the norm that the dignity of the human being should not be violated. It is possible to do so

10 The institutional understanding has been applied to the law by Donald Neil MacCormick (1941-2009) and Ota Weinberger (1919-2009), cf. Institutional Theory, esp. Introduction, pp. 1-30, and Chapter 2, "The Law as an Institutional Fact", pp. 49-76. It has been applied with qualifications by Searle to human rights in Making the Social World, Chapter 8, pp. 174-198. I am expanding this institutional understanding to metaethics, cf. my article, Moral Judgments, but cf. now my remarks on *Sittlichkeit* versus *Morality* on p. 154.

because the proposition itself contains an already built-in norm. "Human dignity is inviolable" also means "Human dignity ought not to be violated." The word "is" in normative contexts has a normative function or force despite its indicative linguistic form.[11]

Thus, facts from all three different worlds – the physical, the psychic and the semantic – can become institutional facts if values and norms are built into them. We can add to facts of all three kinds a normative, evaluative and institutional interpretation.

If these values and norms are of a moral nature, the institutional facts become moral facts. If basic moral facts are of an institutional nature, it is also the case that we can assert the existence of moral facts without contravening "Hume's Law" of the impossibility of deriving an "ought" from an "is". This is so, precisely because such institutional facts contain values and norms from the outset.

From one perspective, the institutional understanding of moral facts can explain the extent to which moral facts are objective and at the same time generalisable. As facts, they are objective and binding for everybody, albeit only in the weak sense of "objective". They are intersubjective or objective within the context of the language community. Such language community today comprises (at least for basic moral facts) the official language of almost all states, and it is codified in the *Universal Declaration of Human Rights*. There is almost no state and hardly any individual who would dare to claim officially that genocide or murder (with the exceptions I have mentioned) is morally permissible. The language community here encompasses almost the entire community of human beings.

From another perspective, this interpretation of moral facts as institutional facts can also explain the extent to which basic moral facts contain a subjective element and moral norms can be derived from them.[12] Basic moral facts contain a subjective element insofar as they are made by a specific language community by means of constitutive rules. It is possible to derive norms from them, since they contain norms from the outset. Thus, from the institutional fact that it is morally right to dress a bleeding wound, but wrong to let the person bleed to death, we can derive the norm that a bleeding wound should be dressed and the person should not be allowed to bleed to death.

---

11 For the normative "is", cf. my article, *"Normatives 'ist' und konstatives 'soll'"*, pp. 185-199.

12 This has been made explicit pace Searle, Speech Acts, p. 179, in my paper, *Moral Judgments*, pp. 722-723.

The institutional understanding of moral facts also explains to what extent moral facts are made and sanctioned by human beings. Institutional facts are obviously made by human beings. From the outset, they contain norms which, if not followed, will entail sanctions. This sanctioning is particularly noticeable where moral facts are institutionalised by law, that is, when they are backed by the state as the sole legitimate bearer of physical violence. The ban on killing (with the exceptions I have so far mentioned) is, for example, enshrined in law. Disregarding this ban – depending on whether it is a question of murder, manslaughter, intentional homicide or homicide caused by negligence – results in a graduated range of fixed punishments such as a fine, prison and, in some states, even the death penalty. Yet, not all institutional facts of a moral nature are legally sanctioned. Nor are all institutional facts sanctioned by law moral. For example, the German law authorising the murder of the mentally handicapped and the ill, brought into force by Hitler through a secret directive, was certainly not moral. Under National Socialism, those who perpetrated acts of this kind did not find themselves in conflict with the law, but were certainly despised by most of their fellow humans and, after the fall of the Third Reich, pursued by the authorities.

Some facts of a basic moral nature are not, or are only moderately, sanctioned by the state. One example of this would be the expectation that we should behave in a friendly and helpful way towards our fellow humans. Such a fact is sanctioned by human beings via means of praise for friendly and helpful behaviour and censure for unfriendly and unhelpful behaviour. Here, while the sanctions are not applied by the state, they are nevertheless of a social nature, consisting in certain positive or negative responses from other people, such as praise or blame, recognition or rejection, and support or obstruction.

Finally, the institutional view of moral facts shows the extent of the demands that these facts can make on me beyond the pursuit of my own interests. The demands of morality as a social institution do not always correspond to what I want. In some cases, I would prefer not to be "moral". Nor is morality as a social institution what God or a metaphysical or supernatural authority expects from me. To believe that, we would have to be able to assume that such an authority, or God, exists. Morality is primarily what a (or *the*) community of human beings demands from me. Since it is not my will, but the will of others that lies behind morality as a social institution, it can demand that I perform certain actions that are not in my own interest but that are in the interest of others.

As a rule, our basic moral feelings are embedded within this framework of institutional facts. They are not simply subjective, but usually well socialised. They internalise the constitutive rules and thereby the will of a language community. We are repelled by a premeditated murder because that is how we were trained to feel by our parents, teachers and fellow humans, and because other people feel the same way. If we had been socialised three thousand (or perhaps even just three hundred) years ago, many or even most of us would be outraged by the murder of a member of our own family, tribe or nation, but perhaps indifferent to, or even satisfied by, the murder of a member of another family, tribe or nation.

The same principle applies to discrimination against people on account of their race, gender, disability, sexual orientation or religion. We regard discrimination on the basis of race, gender, disability, sexual orientation or religion as reprehensible because this is how we were socialised and how we internalised the corresponding constitutive rules. If we had lived in another epoch, many or even most of us would have seen nothing reprehensible about insulting people of a different skin colour, women, and disabled or gay or Jewish people. The institutional view of moral facts can also show how moral laws can evolve and change over time and become more inclusive. Once a language community has fixed these institutional facts, we can apply descriptive propositions to them and, in the process, recognise that murder, or racial or gender discrimination, is reprehensible, as is discrimination on the basis of disability, sexual orientation or religion. Yet, even having done so, we do not see these recognized facts as facts that exist as such, but rather as institutional facts created by human beings.

As a rule, then, while our basic moral feelings are not merely subjective, neither are our basic moral insights strictly objective. Rather, moral emotions and cognitions are inserted into the institutional framework of a community – a framework that is both objective and subjective. It is objective insofar as it exists intersubjectively and regardless of whether or not I recognise it. It is subjective because it has come into being through constitutive rules from which more norms can be derived.

Yet, since the institution of basic morality has largely solidified, it has the appearance of something objectively given. It is so deeply rooted that its human and social origin has been forgotten. This appearance of objectivity is, in fact, necessary for the moral basic rules to be universally recognised and, to a certain degree, to actually be effective.

3. *Normative Ethics*

a) The Concept of the Good as the Foundation of Morality

But why should we be moral? In the previous chapter, we simply accepted that it is morally better, or more correct, not to discriminate against people on account of their race, gender, disability or sexual orientation. In the above examples, we relied even more on an intuitive understanding of what is morally right or wrong when we described dressing a bleeding wound as morally right. Just as we all somehow know the meaning of "is" and "is not", so, too, do we know the meaning of morally "good" and "bad" or "right" and "wrong", and it stands before us to turn this unconscious knowledge into conscious knowledge.

Since the concept of the good also has an action-guiding function, we may hope that the answer to the question "What is morally good?" will also help us to find an answer to the question "Why should we be morally good?" or "Why should we act in the morally right way?" This is the task of normative ethics.

In order to arrive at an answer to this question by means of elucidating the concept of the good, it is simply not enough to give a *cause* as to why we should act in the right way. If we were to give a cause, it could be an inner trigger or a motive, for example, fear or hope – such as hope of a reward for a good deed and fear of punishment for a bad deed. We would, of course, prefer to be rewarded rather than punished. If we were always rewarded for moral behaviour and always punished for immoral behaviour, moral behaviour would be synonymous with what we wanted on behalf of ourselves. The kind of behaviour which cleverly pursues our own interests is also called being "wise" in the sense of *prudent.*

Obviously, it is prudent to behave in such a way that we are rewarded and imprudent to behave in such a way that we are punished. Often, moral behaviour is prudent, and goodness is the best policy. Yet, this is not always the case. Occasionally, moral behaviour is imprudent. Our own goodness is at times the most formidable weapon in the hands of our enemies. Our goodness is often not rewarded, but rather exploited and punished. Again and again, it is in fact wickedness that is rewarded. We all know that the "bad guys" are sometimes rewarded and the "good guys" sometimes punished, even though we cannot put it quite like Shakespeare: "Some rise by sin and some by virtue fall."[13]

---

13 *Measure for Measure*, Escalus, Act 2, Scene 1.

Therefore, in reply to the question “Why should we be good and act in the right way?”, we cannot invoke a *cause* or personal *motive* – for example, our own self-interest – and say “We should be good, that is, act in the right way, because it is in our own self-interest”. Rather, we look for a *reason* to be good or to act in the right way. But this reason should be independent of any concern about rewards and punishments.

Morality, as a social institution, is an institution supported by social sanctions. Otherwise, it would be basically ineffective. But rewards and punishments do not account for the validity of morality. Although social sanctions are often the motives for our moral behaviour, they are not the *reason* that we should behave morally. Beyond a certain level of social evolution, we have internalised the institutions of morality so deeply that it commands us to be moral, even if we are neither rewarded for moral behaviour nor punished for immoral behaviour. Moral behaviour resembles a steamship that continues to coast along long after the engines of self-interest have been cut.

Yet, only then do we believe that we are acting in a truly moral way, once we have abandoned our self-interest and ceased to expect anything in return. The searched definition of the good tries to give a *reason* for why we should be moral and act morally, even in the absence of a reward. Such a *reason* can become nevertheless an *indirect cause* guiding our actions. The reason for morality becomes the cause if we adopt it and allow it to determine our actions. It is this reason that we seek in the concept of the moral good.

b) The Good as Utility

In what follows, I therefore take the concept of the good and the bad as my starting point, ignoring motives such as (external) reward and punishment. From our institutionalist position, I will restrict the question “What is morally good?” to “Which institutional facts are morally good?” In order to arrive at an answer, we will first consider the consequences of the morally good and the morally bad (or evil). In order to do so, we shall start with the following statement by Plato: “The bad is all that destroys and corrupts, and the good is all that saves and benefits.”[14]

Plato does not yet distinguish here between what is good in itself and what is good only as a means to an end. He believes that everything that is good

---

14 Plato, R., Book 10, 608 e. My translation.

saves and benefits, while everything that is bad corrupts and destroys. Therefore, the morally good also saves and benefits, while the morally bad also corrupts and destroys.

To put it more simply: The morally good is *useful*, while the morally bad is *harmful*. It is morally *wrong not* to dress a bleeding wound because that harms the injured person who would otherwise bleed to death. But it is morally *right* to dress the wound, because this action benefits the bleeding person. Genocide is even more morally wrong because it leads to the destruction of a whole people. But supplying food is morally right, because it preserves life. Morality, then, is generally useful and life advancing, immorality harmful and life obstructing. Indeed, morality as a social institution would have found it hard to establish and consolidate itself if, in contrast to immorality, it was not beneficial – at least for the life of the community, if not always for the life of each individual.

The definition "The good is life enhancing and the bad life obstructing" provides the following answer to the question of why we should be good and act in the right way: Morally right actions are useful and life enhancing; morally wrong actions are harmful and life obstructing. Therefore, the reason for morality is an extramoral value, namely, usefulness or the ability to enhance life. Accordingly, those institutional facts that are useful and life enhancing are morally right, and those that are harmful and life obstructing are morally wrong.

We do not, however, simply want to live. We want to live happily, and we do not want to live unhappily. If we were asked to describe the difference between a happy life and an unhappy life, we might answer that a happy life is full of pleasure and an unhappy life full of pain. According to this view, morality is not only life enhancing, and immorality is not only life obstructing, but morality actually leads to a happy or pleasurable life and immorality to an unhappy or painful one.

This sounds strange because the term "moral" today has acquired a secondary meaning of being the enemy of pleasure. Nevertheless, it is a view that has been asserted time and again from Greek antiquity down to the present day. It is called "eudemonism" (from *eudaímonía*: happiness) and "hedonism" (from *hēdoné*: pleasure). An influential newer version of this theory is found in John Stuart Mill's *Utilitarianism* (1863), where both eudemonism and hedonism are bracketed under the concept of "utilitarianism" (from *utilitas*: usefulness):

> The creed which accepts as the foundation of morals, Utility, or the Greatest Happiness Principle, holds that actions are right in proportion as they tend to promote happiness, wrong as they tend to produce

> the reverse of happiness. By happiness is intended pleasure, and the absence of pain; by unhappiness, pain, and the privation of pleasure.[15]

Since Mill has actions in mind, we can also refer to this as "act utilitarianism": A single action – such as dressing the wound of a person about to bleed to death – is morally right if it promotes happiness or pleasure; it is wrong if it causes the opposite of happiness or pleasure, that is, unhappiness or pain. Utilitarianism can further be extended to include rules. Hence, we can also talk about "rule utilitarianism": A rule – for example, "Thou shalt not kill" – is morally right if it generates happiness or pleasure and morally wrong if it causes misfortune or suffering.

Among these rules, we may include not only regulative moral precepts, such as "Thou shalt not kill", but also constitutive moral rules, such as "A certain action X is regarded as morally right in the context of the language community LC". Since rules of this kind are absorbed into institutional facts, we may, within our institutionalist position, expand rule utilitarianism into institutional utilitarianism. Institutional utilitarianism, like rule utilitarianism but unlike act utilitarianism, can fall back on the moral tradition of the basic rules and institutions discussed so far, the consequences of which are to a large extent known to us from experience. This is simpler than having to consider afresh before each individual action what the consequences would be. Existing moral institutions were established through a lengthy process, and we may assume that they are not completely wrong. But this does not give any sufficient reason to think that all existing institutional facts *per se* are morally right.

Institutional utilitarianism supplies us with a criterion for determining when institutional facts are morally right or wrong. Institutional facts are morally right if they generate happiness, pleasure or utility and morally wrong if they generate unhappiness, pain or harm. Thus, for example, the institutional fact that "Human dignity is inviolable" is morally right because it generates happiness, pleasure or utility. The opposite is morally wrong because it generates unhappiness, pain or damage. Further, the institutional fact that "magnanimity is good, envy is wrong" is morally right because magnanimity, as a rule, leads to happiness, pleasure or utility, and envy leads to unhappiness, pain and harm – not only for the object of the envy, but also for the envious subject. As has been said, envy is the only vice that has no pleasure in it.

15 Mill, Utilitarianism, Chapter 2, pp. 9-10.

It is important to note that utilitarianism does not claim that those actions or institutions alone are good that enhance my happiness, pleasure and utility. It does not claim that what is good is what benefits only me, but also thinks of others. Modern utilitarianism also does not distinguish between different social levels. It does not say that what is good is what benefits my class only and in the best case indirectly the others. Modern utilitarianism is democratic. It believes that the good is what maximises the happiness, pleasure or utility of as many human beings as possible. In this process, according to a formula by Jeremy Bentham (1748-1832), "everybody [is] to count for one, and nobody for more than one". This is so because everybody's basic interests are equal to everybody else's. The good, then, phrased in a catchy way, is what brings "the greatest possible happiness to the greatest possible number of people". The good is what maximises the happiness, pleasure or utility of the greatest possible number of people.

By appealing to this criterion, I can also explain why discrimination on the basis of race, gender, sexual orientation or disability is morally wrong and non-discrimination right. Imagine the great pleasure food can give to a hungry person and the appalling pain experienced by somebody starving to death. We feel a similar pain if, for example, we are rejected when looking for a job or an apartment, or if we are disadvantaged or unfairly treated in some other way because of our race, gender, religion, sexual orientation or disability.

Institutions and institutional facts that discriminate are also morally wrong because they do not contribute to the greatest happiness, or greatest pleasure, of the greatest number and may actually cause the majority of people unhappiness or pain. Thus, the criterion of utilitarianism reveals not only when institutions are good, but also when they are fair. Fairness here means equal treatment of people of different race, gender, ability, sexual orientation and religion. Fairness is what maximises the happiness, pleasure or utility of the majority or, in the ideal case, of all concerned. With happiness, pleasure or utility as its purpose, morality as understood by utilitarianism is built on an extramoral value.

If we ask for proof of the thesis that the good is happiness, pleasure or utility, we receive the following answer: Everybody strives for happiness, pleasure and utility. Seventeen-year-old Cécile in Françoise Sagan's novel *Bonjour Tristesse* confesses candidly: "My love of pleasure seems to be the only consistent side of my character." It is because everybody strives to be happy that everybody regards happiness, pleasure and utility as good. That is why eudemonism, hedonism and utilitarianism, in both theory and practice, are recognised by everybody. Mill writes:

> If the end which the utilitarian doctrine proposes to itself were not, in theory and in practice, acknowledged to be an end, nothing could ever convince any person that it was so. No reason can be given why the general happiness is desirable, except that each person, so far as he believes it to be attainable, desires his own happiness. This, however, being a fact, we have not only all the proof which the case admits of, but all which it is possible to require, that happiness is a good: that each person's happiness is a good to that person, and the general happiness, therefore, a good to the aggregate of all persons.[16]

"All the proof which the case admits of" is no proof at all in the strict sense. It does not prove the thesis by deriving it as a conclusion from certain premises. Rather, it confers on the thesis itself the status of a first premise or axiom. Just as it is evident that an object is visible if we actually see it, it is equally evident that we all want our own happiness, our own pleasure and our own utility. What we want we regard as good. Thus, we all regard our own happiness, our own pleasure and our own utility as good. To that extent, Mill shares the classic definition of good as "that at which all things aim". But from the axiom of utilitarianism, he draws the conclusion that the purpose of the utilitarian theory is also right in that everybody regards universal happiness as desirable, that is, as good, and that everybody desires universal happiness.

As we have seen, evidence is only a prima facie criterion for the truth of an axiom. Therefore, it is also only a prima facie argument in favour of the axiom of utilitarianism. On reflection, some objections arise. They concern both the axiom of utilitarianism and the validity of the argument based on the axiom. Let us first consider the validity of the argument.

α) Let us assume that this axiom is evident and that we all want our own happiness, pleasure or utility and therefore regard our own happiness, pleasure and utility as good. But, from this premise, the conclusion does not follow that we all also want the happiness, pleasure or utility of others and also regard the happiness, pleasure or utility of others as good. It also follows even less that we all want, or regard as good, the greatest possible happiness, pleasure and utility of the greatest possible number of other people. Yet, if moral actions and institutions are supposed to promote "the greatest happiness of the greatest number", they will not only serve my

16 Mill, Utilitarianism, Chapter 4, pp. 52-53.

happiness, but also the happiness of others. As we have seen, moral institutions can demand actions from me that go beyond my own interests. It is not immediately obvious how, by wanting my own happiness and regarding it as good, I also want and regard as good the "happiness of the greatest number".

β) The argument of utilitarianism may be invalid, while its axiom is, at the same time, true. The axiom that we all want (and regard as good) our own happiness, pleasure or utility seems evident. But opinions differ as to what our own happiness, pleasure or utility actually is. If we were to replace the general terms "happiness", "pleasure" or "utility" with the concrete ideas that people mean by them, we would end up with very different things, such as those dying of thirst long for a glass of water, those who are very hungry long for a slice of bread, those who are freezing long for a warm coat, those without a home long for a roof over their heads, those confined to a dark prison long for sunshine and freedom, those who are lonely long for a human companion, or those surrounded by too many people long for solitude. In addition, it is also possible to want to give pleasure to others. The axiom of utilitarianism seems so evident only because it does not say exactly what people want. If we cut to the heart of the matter, it says very little or nothing.

Another way of putting this point would be to say that we all desire something desirable. Yet, this change of wording shows that the axiom of utilitarianism is not an empirical hypothesis that can be falsified through experience. It is a conceptual thesis that is true only on the basis of the meaning of the words used. On the basis of the meaning of the words "desire" and "desirable", it is true that we all desire desirable things. Yet, as true as this axiom is, it is also tautological and trivial. As soon as we formulate it as an empirical hypothesis, it becomes false. We do not desire happiness, pleasure or utility directly. Not only do we desire good things in general, but we obviously desire *different* good things *according to our needs*. Yet, only once we abstract from the individual goods and ask ourselves what we desire to achieve through them, can we say, in hindsight, that we were desiring happiness, pleasure or utility. Therefore, the axiom of utilitarianism only *seems to be* directly evident. In reality, it rests on *acquired* evidence, and this acquired evidence can also be called into question through reflection. Seen up close, it is actually false.

γ) Hence, we see that the conclusion of utilitarianism does not follow from the axiom of utilitarianism and that the axiom of utilitarianism is not directly evident. Yet, even if the axiom of utilitarianism were directly evident and if the "end which the utilitarian doctrine proposes to itself" followed from it, we could still ask: Is my happiness, pleasure or utility morally good? Is even the greatest possible happiness, pleasure or utility of the greatest possible number morally good?

I must answer these questions in the negative, just as I already answered the question of whether everything that everybody aims at is morally good (cf. p. 125). The utilitarian definition of good – like the classic definition of good as "that at which all things aim" – does not distinguish between the morally good and the extramorally good. Even if happiness, pleasure and utility are good, this does not mean that they are morally good from the outset. This is true of both my happiness and the happiness of others because it is also possible to aim at making others happy in a way which is regarded as immoral, such as if we were to aid and abet in a murder. Likewise, our own happiness is by no means always morally good *per se* – such as when it rests on the misfortune of others, for example.

As we have seen, the morally good is not something that we can perceive by means of an external experience, as we are able to do in the case of perceiving colours or sounds, for example. Nor is it something that we can perceive directly within us by means of an internal experience, as we are able to do in the case of pleasure or pain, for example. What is morally good is not a real predicate and has no real existence. It is determined through constitutive semantic rules and therefore has only semantic existence. The semantic rules in question spring from the basic will of a community and are absorbed by the institutional facts of that community. After the event, however, they can be internalised by the individual. Thus, the concept of the morally good acquires a dimension that is not exhausted by the eudemonistic, hedonistic and utilitarian definitions. At the same time, it is a mistake of eudemonism, hedonism and Mill's utilitarianism to explain the concept of the morally good by means of other concepts (such as happiness, pleasure or utility) which do not automatically contain this moral dimension. Along with G. E. Moore, we can call this mistake the "naturalistic fallacy" or, in the terminology of the previous chapter, the "realistic fallacy".[17] It consists in the immediate transition from a "natural" or real predicate – happiness, pleasure or utility – to a semantic one, that is, that of the morally good.

---

17 Moore, PE, Chapter 1, § 10: "But far too many philosophers have thought that when they named those other properties they were actually defining good; that these properties, in fact, were simply not 'other,' but absolutely and entirely the same with goodness. This view I propose to call the 'naturalistic fallacy' and of it I shall now endeavour to dispose."

This "naturalistic" or "realistic" fallacy is the ontological counterpart to the logical fallacy of inferring a normative statement from a constative one (cf. pp. 129-130). Just as little as I can infer a normative statement from a constative one, can I infer a semantic predicate from a real one. Not only does the content of a normative statement go beyond that of a constative one, but the content of a semantic predicate also exceeds that of a real one. We need a rule that tells us *how far* a real fact that promotes happiness, pleasure or utility is morally good. In contrast, any rules that aimed at happiness, pleasure or utility would turn the comparatively absolute character of moral obligation into something relative by making it dependent on an extra-moral condition, that is, the condition of the happiness, pleasure or utility of the greatest possible number. Moore was right to place Joseph Butler's dictum as a motto at the head of his *Principia Ethica*: "Everything is what it is and not another thing" (cf. p. 65). Thus, the morally good, too, is what it is and no other "thing" such as happiness, pleasure or utility.

But even if happiness, pleasure or utility were the condition for the rightness of our moral institutions, it would be difficult to define positively what this condition could be. Happiness can mean different things to different people, such that it is not easy to compare the happiness of different people. This is all the more true if we leave it to people to decide for themselves what to see, and look for, as their happiness. Different people look for different things in seeking happiness (although most of them may agree on what misfortune is, such as poverty, illness and death.) Yet, they often do not really know what they are looking for. They resemble drunks looking for their houses with the vague idea that they have one.[18] Sometimes they are not even looking for a house, but only for a castle in the air. Happiness, to borrow a definition used by Kant in another context, is an "ideal of imagination".[19] The "greatest happiness of the greatest number" is even more an "ideal of imagination".

Happiness cannot be pursued directly, as Aristotle saw it rightly, but rather completes an activity like "an end which supervenes as beauty does on those in the flower of their age".[20] Real, "profound happiness", however, insofar as it is accessible, may, in Spengler's words, be "presence without thought".[21]

---

18 This saying is attributed to Voltaire.

19 Kant, Groundwork, Section 2, p. 418.

20 Aristotle, NE, Book 10, Chapter 4, 1174b33. My translation.

21 Spengler, Urfragen, Chapter XI, fragment 41, p. 321.

c) The Good as a Rule

Hence, it is advisable to look for a more correct answer to the question "What is morally good?" We already used this answer in an undeveloped form when we characterised basic moral propositions as generalisable. But utilitarianism likewise assumes this answer in an undeveloped form. It does so insofar as it sees the good in the happiness of others, that is, "the greatest happiness of the greatest number", formulating the *rule* that every human being must be counted as one human being and no human being as more than one. This answer is also to be found (again in an undeveloped form) in the Sermon on the Mount where Jesus commands: "Therefore all things whatever ye would that men should do to you, do ye even so to them."[22]

This rule is called the *Golden Rule*. It can be phrased positively or negatively. The wording found in the Sermon on the Mount is positive. The negative wording that has become established is "Don't do to others what you don't want others to do to you".

The Golden Rule was developed by Kant. In his view, the morally good is not happiness, nor is it the "greatest happiness of the greatest number". We are told what is morally good by rules. Among the relevant rules, there is one main rule, that is, the rule of generalisation. Kant calls this rule the "categorical imperative". Although in his *Groundwork of the Metaphysics of Morals* (1783) Kant formulates it in different ways, it remains, in his words, "but one categorical imperative":

> There is therefore but one categorical imperative, namely, this: *Act only on that maxim whereby thou canst at the same time will that it should become a universal law.*[23]

Kant calls this imperative "categorical" because, in contrast to a hypothetical imperative, it is not relative or conditional, but absolute and unconditional. In particular, it is not tied to the condition of happiness, pleasure or utility. It is free of the consequences that could result for me and others who follow it. We can foresee these consequences to a great extent, but not

---

22 Matthew, VII, 12. Transl. King James Bible. Cf. Luke 6, 31. Worded negatively, the Golden Rule is already found in Tobit, 4, 15 of the Old Testament: "What you hate, do not do to any one" and in Confucius, Lunyu 15, 24: "Zu-kung asked saying, 'Is there any single saying that one can act upon all day and every day?'. The Master said, 'Isn't it *shù*?' 'What you do not want yourself, don't do to [other] human beings (*ren*).'" (Transl. Legge with modification due to H. v. Senger).

23 Kant, Groundwork, Section 2, p. 491. Transl. Gregor. Emphasis in the original.

always. Nevertheless, we must abide by this rule and simply wait for what may come: "One must be Good and expect the rest."[24]

The categorical imperative tells us that any action is good only if it is carried out according to maxims that can be generalised. A maxim is a subjective principle. Therefore, the categorical imperative demands that we act only on those subjective principles that are generalisable. A subjective principle is generalisable if we all are able to adopt it without willing something that we cannot will. Subjective principles, which everybody is able to adopt, can be valid on the intersubjective level. Therefore, the categorical imperative commands us to act only on those subjective principles that can be valid at the intersubjective level.

Within our institutionalist position, we may also expand this rule of the generalisability of our actions to institutional facts: The only morally right institutional facts are those that all other people can adopt as far as possible. Thus, the criterion of generalisability, which was developed above for moral basic propositions, also becomes the reason that they are morally right.

By this criterion, we can explain why, for example, the institutional fact of dressing a bleeding wound is good, while letting a person bleed to death is bad, or saving people from starvation is good, but genocide bad. Such institutional facts are clearly generalisable: I can will a law that commands us to dress a bleeding wound, but forbids us to let a person bleed to death, or a law that orders us to save people from starving to death, but forbids genocide. However, I cannot will a general law that forbids us to dress a bleeding wound, but allows us to let a person bleed to death. Even less can I will a law that forbids saving people from starvation, but permits genocide. If I willed such a law, I would implicitly will something that I cannot explicitly will. After all, I myself could one day be in danger of bleeding or starving to death, or indeed of being murdered. But generally, I can no more will to bleed or starve to death than I can will to be murdered. Given such a law, I would find myself in a conflict of my will.

By the same criterion, we can also explain why discrimination against people because of their race, gender, sexual orientation, disability or religion is morally wrong and non-discrimination is right. Non-discrimination is right because this institutional fact is generalisable, while discrimination is not. Let us assume that there is a general law that allows discrimination against a race, gender, sexual orientation, disability or religion. This would mean that, just as I would be allowed to discriminate against other people

24 Kant, Observations, p. 19. "Good" capitalized in German. Transl. Frierson/Guyer.

because of their race, gender, sexual orientation, disability and religion, other people would be allowed to discriminate against me because of my race, gender, sexual orientation, disability and religion. But if I willed a law that allowed me to be discriminated against, I would will something that I cannot will. I cannot will to be discriminated against.

I can no more deny the metalogical axioms of identity and non-contradiction than I can will the "moral axioms" themselves to be abolished. I cannot deny the metalogical axioms of identity and contradiction because, in order to deny them, I must affirm them (cf. pp. 67-68). Yet, in order to abolish "moral axioms" such as the ban on killing or discrimination, I would have to will something that I cannot will. In the first instance, I would be caught up in a contradiction (*Widerspruch*) in my language and theoretical reason. In the second instance, I would be caught up in a conflict (*Widerstreit*) of my practical reason or, to put it differently, in a conflict of my reasonable will.

This position, which claims to be able to tell what is right and wrong on the basis of the generalisation rule, is not called utilitarian. Rather, this position is called "deontological" (from *to déon*: that which is binding) because these commands impose an obligation on us regardless of any useful consequences they may have. Likewise, the main imperative, that is, the obligation to generalise, exists regardless of any useful consequences it may have. In fact, there is no necessary connection between my moral or immoral behaviour and the outcome of this behaviour. This is why there is also no necessary connection between the concepts of morality and happiness or between the concepts of immorality and unhappiness. Moral behaviour often, but not necessarily, leads to happiness, and immoral behaviour often, but not necessarily, leads to unhappiness. Happiness (*Glückseligkeit*) can be an addition to moral behaviour and "blossom unexpectedly", but it need not be so. Moral behaviour may lead essentially only to something "analogous" to happiness, that is, "self-contentment" (*Selbstzufriedenheit*)[25] – at least for those who consider moral behaviour a part of being content with themselves.

One merit of the deontological position is that, unlike the hedonistic, eudemonistic or utilitarian positions, it sees no conceptual link between morality and happiness but instead makes this connection dependent on the way of the world. Another merit of the deontological position is that it does not commit the "naturalistic" or "realistic fallacy". It explains the con-

25 Cf. Kant, CPrR AA, p. 212.

cept of the morally good not by means of the real consequences that can be experienced internally or externally, but by means of a rule of our will.
However, the generalisation rule – regardless of the different wordings found in Kant – is also open to serious objections. Three remarks about the generalisation rule concerning institutional facts must suffice here:
α) First, the generalisation rule, which determines what is good or bad, starts with a prior understanding of what is morally good or bad. Not every maxim that can be generalised is morally good by definition. What if we wanted a general law that obliged everybody to get up early in the morning? Would that make getting up early a morally relevant action?
The generalisation rule alone, then, cannot furnish us with the criterion necessary to determine whether some institutional facts are morally right or wrong. Morally indifferent institutional facts could also be transformed into duties for everyone. To be able to serve as a criterion, the generalisation rule requires certain initial guidelines about what is prima facie morally good and what is wrong. After all, it is this rule that makes the criterion of moral institutional facts the foundation of morality.
It is a particular characteristic of these guidelines that the only actions to be institutionalised are those that have direct or indirect consequences for the vital interests of other people. Morality, *as defined here*, is, in the first instance, social morality. Getting up early would be morally relevant only if the vital interests of other people were directly or indirectly affected by it. They would be affected if they suffered an undeserved disadvantage owing to my getting up late – as would be the case, for example, when an emergency doctor arrived late to the scene of an accident, violating the moral imperative to save life.
Hence, it is only if we are guided by a prior understanding of which institutional facts are moral that the generalisation rule provides a criterion as to when an institutional fact is morally right. This shows us that the generalisation rule cannot on its own determine which facts are moral, but can do so only in connection with a prior understanding of what is morally good. This would involve taking the consequences of the good and the bad into account, and is basically utilitarian. Following what has been said above, getting up early is a morally relevant action if it has either useful or harmful consequences for the vital interests of other people.
β) Second, the generalisation rule assumes that, just as my actions can have either a positive or a negative effect on the vital interests of other people, the actions of others must be able to either positively or negatively affect my vital interests. Usually, none of us is so far removed from other people as to hope or fear nothing from them. If we had nothing to hope or fear

from other people, we would be able to generalise our subjective principles without a conflict of our will. Thus, the generalisation rule does not apply independent of all experience. It is only valid under specific conditions and, in particular, under the condition of a certain uniformity of people and their circumstances. These conditions are, however, such that we can regard them as largely fulfilled by most institutional facts of a moral nature. None of us is protected from others to such a degree that we could not be killed, robbed, defrauded, abused or otherwise disadvantaged.
γ) Finally, the generalisation rule does not exist in isolation from all consequences either, but rather also takes account of the consequences that certain institutions of a moral nature may have. The generalisation rule is predicated on the fact that I cannot want the consequences of its abolition. I cannot want an institution that allows killing without restraint, because I myself do not want to be killed. However, the generalisation rule considers not only the consequences that its abolition could have for me, but also the consequences that it could have for others. It abstracts from my vital interests and takes account of the vital interests of all others by equating mine with theirs.
The *categorical* imperative, then, is in principle a *hypothetical* imperative that makes the vital interests of all people the condition of morality. It is a general hypothetical imperative, which could be worded as follows: Act solely on that principle which considers not only your vital interests, but those of *all* other people. And this means that as much as Mill and Kant may differ in their reasoning, they agree on the aim. Mill himself put this as follows:

> To give any meaning to Kant's principle, the sense put upon it must be, that we ought to shape our conduct by a rule which all rational beings might adopt with benefit to their collective interest.[26]

Thus, neither the prerequisites nor the aims of the utilitarian and the deontological positions are as far apart as they seem to be. Both are guided by a prior understanding of the good that takes the consequences into account. Both aim at useful consequences, not only for me, but also for all other people.
Nevertheless, the deontological explanation of morality is clearly preferable to the utilitarian one because it makes it clear that the morally good is not necessarily connected with the concept of happiness, pleasure or utility, but rather presupposes a specific will. The specific will, according to

26 Mill, Utilitarianism, Chapter 5, pp. 78-79.

this interpretation, is the will of a human community. Constitutive moral rules and the institutional facts corresponding to them are facts for a human community. One aspect of an institutional fact is that it applies to every member of a specific language community, LC. The criterion of morality suggested here indicates only that the language community LC must not be restricted to a specific group LC_1, LC_2, LC_3, etc. – for example, rich, white, protestant men, etc. – but should, as far as possible, include all people.

With these reservations, we can accept the generalisation rule not as a law, but as a rule of thumb and define it as follows: Morally right, or good, institutional facts are those that affect the vital interests of other people and that can, in principle, be adopted by all of us without wanting anything that we cannot want. Conversely, morally wrong, or bad, institutional facts are those that affect the vital interests of other people and that cannot be adopted by all of us because, in so doing, we would have to want something that we cannot want.

The vital interests of other people can be understood in a narrower and in a broader sense. In the narrower sense, they refer to basic, undamaged life. In the broader sense, they refer to a free, equal and happy life. Thus, the ban on killing, for example, is morally right because it concerns the interest of other people in basic life and because it can be adopted by everyone without a conflict of the will. The ban on discrimination is morally right because it touches on other people's interest in a free and equal life and because, again, we can all adopt it without conflict.

Therefore, metaethical institutionalism does not lead into moral relativism. Moral relativism we may define with Plato in the following way:

> Whatever in any city is regarded as just and admirable, *is* just and admirable, in that city and for so long as that convention maintains itself.[27]

When, for example, a city or country regards slavery as just and admirable, then it *is* just and admirable in this city or country. The same would be true concerning discrimination of people on the basis of race, gender, sexual orientation and disability or religion.

Metaethical institutionalism marks, with the generalisation rule, the *dividing line* between moral and immoral institutional facts. So it is an immoral institutional fact that some human beings are treated as slaves because it

27 Tht. 167 c. Transl. Levett, rev. Burneyat.

cannot in principle be adopted by all of us without wanting something that we cannot want, etc.

In such a way, the proposed institutionalism tries also to give a *synthesis* of morality and legality. With the generalisation rule, institutionalism provides a moral foundation for legal obligations. Moral obligations which are not embedded in the laws of the state or, at least, in the customs of a community, very often, if not always, remain inefficient. This can be observed when, as in war, some laws of the state or the community (such as those against stealing or treating other people as slaves) are no longer in force. At the same time, legal obligations without moral foundation are not yet moral. It is not yet a moral achievement not to steal only because the state or the community that I live in has forbidden stealing and I fear the sanctions that may result. It becomes a moral act only when I am tempted to steal, but do not steal, because I think it is right not to steal although I do not have to fear any sanctions.

The *synthesis* of morality and legality has been called by Hegel *Sittlichkeit* in distinction to (reflective) *morality*.[28] Thus, institutionalism also tries to redefine what Hegel called *Sittlichkeit*, that is, customary or institutional morality, mirrored in everyday mores, in distinction from (reflected) *morality*. *Sittlichkeit* may be defined as the free acceptance and observation of the prevailing institutions of the community that I live in (insofar, I would add, as they are legitimated by the generalisation rule). *Morality* for Hegel, in distinction to *Sittlichkeit*, is the reflected morality of my personal consciousness and may go beyond customary or institutional morality.

It is, for example, a legal obligation not to steal money from my mother or father with dementia but to support them financially if necessary. It is a still widely accepted institutional obligation of *Sittlichkeit* to give them a gift at Christmas, or not to forget their birthday or, at least, to be present at their funeral, if possible. But it is a reflected personal *moral* obligation to pay them a visit once a week.

The generalisation rule is not a strict law, however, but only a rule of thumb, because its application requires "power of judgment sharpened by experience", as Kant says about moral laws in general.[29] The power of judgment is a faculty of common sense. One of its tasks is to determine which individual cases fall under a given rule. Aristotle illustrates this with the following extra-moral example:

---

28 Hegel, Philosophy of Right, Part 3, § 142.

29 Kant, Groundwork, Foreword, p. 389. Transl. Gregor.

> This is why some who do not have knowledge, and especially those who have experience, are more practical than others who have knowledge; for if a man knew that light meats are digestible and wholesome, but did not know which sorts of meat are light, he would not be promoting his health, but the man who knows that chicken is wholesome is more likely to be promoting his health.[30]

It is the power of judgment that decides which meat benefits our health or at least does not upset our digestion.

Similarly, it could be said that if we know that discrimination should be avoided, but perhaps not when a person of another skin colour, gender, sexual orientation, disability or religion will feel discriminated against, we shall not accomplish a great deal as a result of this general knowledge. We are more likely to achieve something if we also know when a person will feel discriminated against or hurt. Some people feel discriminated against by the mere mention that they are black or gay or of Jewish or Muslim faith, while others are proud of this fact.

A further task of the power of judgment is to decide how to apply the rule to the individual case. In so doing, it must follow a principle that mediates between the two. We can call this the *principle of the appropriate*. This principle may be paraphrased in various ways. Plato, for example, who did not yet know the generalisation rule, explains this principle as "...the graceful, the opportune, the right, and all that has its seat in the middle between two extreme ends".[31] This "graceful and opportune" is not the ultimate good, that is, it is not the *idea or ideal* of the good, which Plato also calls "the Exact itself", and is to him the ultimate standard of measure.[32] But it shows how "the Exact itself" is to be realised in empirical conditions characterised by a certain inaccuracy.

What is morally right is essentially expressed today in terms of the generalisation rule, and even though we cannot capture the ideal of the good by following it, it must also be applied by using the power of judgment. This is why its use, once again, leads to a certain inaccuracy. We may try to avoid the extremes of discrimination against women and disadvantaging men, but we will not always be able to avoid both at the same time. Likewise, we must apply the rule against lying with judgment. An experienced

---

30 Aristotle, EN, Book 6, Chapter 7. Transl. Ross, slightly modified.

31 Plt. 284 e. Transl. Skemp with modification. For this principle, cf. my article, Propedeutic Lecture of the *Politicus*, esp. pp. 201-206.

32 Plt. 284 d. My translation.

physician, for example, must sometimes withhold the whole truth from a patient, without actually lying.

The poet Ingeborg Bachmann wrote: "People can face the truth." But the truth can be traumatic. Therefore, we must tell it as appropriate, for example, waiting for the right moment, avoiding the extremes of deception and discouragement, and trying not to hurt anyone's feelings.

The principle of the appropriate cannot supply a prescription for dealing with all the isolated incidents of life. Time and again, our power of judgment has to mediate afresh between the generalisation rule and the individual incidents, paying attention to the demands of the appropriate. The use of this rule allows a certain modification, so that what is appropriate in one situation need not be appropriate in another. Here, the principle of Aristotle applies: "Such things depend on particular facts, and the decision rests with the perception [of the concrete situation]."[33]

4. Minimum and Maximum Morality

The generalisation rule does not explain all institutional facts of a moral nature, but only those that are necessary for minimum institutional morality. By "minimum morality", I mean a morality that adheres to basic moral propositions such as those forbidding killing and discrimination. I was required to take these basic propositions as my starting point because they represent, as it were, the *Urphänomen* of institutional morality.

Morality begins with the ban on killing (and incest). As a result of our profound interest in life itself, the ban on killing carries exceptional weight. Thus, many states today protect even the life of a murderer.

Modern morality is aptly described by the statement that all human beings are created equal and, as human beings, have the same rights. We find this not only in the American Declaration of Independence (1776; cf. p. 78), but also in the Declaration of Human and Civil Rights (1789) of the French National Assembly: "Human beings are born and remain free and equal in rights. Social distinctions may be founded only upon the general good" (Article 1). If human beings are born and remain free and equal in their rights, no human being must be discriminated against as the result of an accidental characteristic, such as race, gender, religion, disability or sexual orientation. Since we also have a profound interest in a free and equal life, the ban on discrimination has likewise been given a very wide remit.

33 EN, Book 2, Chapter 9, 1109b23-24. Transl. Ross.

In contrast to such a *minimum morality*, there is a *maximum morality* which commands us to love our neighbours and even our enemies. This is the morality of the Gospel and, in particular, of the Sermon on the Mount.[34] The command to love our neighbours and our enemies can be generalised without embroiling us in a conflict of will. If all people love their enemies, all of my enemies also love me. This is something that I can obviously will without finding myself in a conflict of will. But, however much we praise those who love – that is, those who sincerely do good to – their enemies, we do not blame those who do not love their enemy. Demands of the kind that call upon us to love our neighbours and our enemies are maximum demands. We could also call them ideals. As ideals, they rise above the concept of morality outlined here, although for smaller communities, for example, communities of Christians and other communities trying to live according to the demands of the Sermon on the Mount, they are binding.

Conversely, merely prudential rules, which only command us to act in our own interest, fall below the concept of institutional morality (as I have sketched it) and indeed belong in the field of eudemonism. Eudemonism tries to show how we can be happy or at least not unhappy. It does not prescribe, in a generally binding way, what we are to do and not to do. Rather, it gives recommendations that we may follow in order to reach a specific goal, that is, happiness or well-being. Such recommendations may either keep within the bounds of morality or violate them.

An example of advice that keeps within the bounds of morality would be Kant's recommendation of "regimen, frugality, courtesy, reserve, etc., which experience teaches do, on the average, most promote well-being".[35] To this recommendation of an austere, aging philosopher I would add Maxim Gorki's statement: "Long live the man who knows not how to be frugal to himself."[36]

In contrast, the prudential rules of unrestrained selfishness that a leader is advised to observe by Niccolò Machiavelli in *The Prince* do not obey morality. "Injuries", says Machiavelli, "ought to be done all at one time, so that, being tasted less, they offend less; benefits ought to be given little by little, so that the flavour of them may last longer."[37]

In these reflections, I have tried to follow a middle way between the demands of maximum morality, on the one hand, and the prudential rules of

34 Cf. Matthew 5.43-44, 22.38; Luke 6.27-30.

35 Kant, Groundwork, Section 2, p. 418. Transl. Gregor.

36 From the story "The Clock", Chapter 8. Transl. Ted Crawford with modification.

37 Machiavelli, Prince, Chapter 8, p. 271. Transl. Marriott.

unlimited selfishness, on the other. The result is a generalisable minimum institutional morality or *Sittlichkeit*, which provides only a few guidelines – such as the "moral axioms" mentioned above – within which we can realise our vital interests and pursue our happiness. No one should do less than what is demanded by such a minimum morality, but everyone may do more and, of course, there is a broad grey area between this minimum morality and a maximal morality.

Those who do more than is demanded by this minimum morality produce meritorious or "supererogatory" (from *supererogare*: paying over the odds) works.[38] Whoever not only pays lip service to the ideals of the Sermon on the Mount, but actually lives by them, can be said to do more than is normally expected. A general practitioner who moves to a distant region in order to develop basic medical services for a poor population, even though he could earn a higher income and have a more comfortable life as a specialist in the city, performs such a praiseworthy deed. Nobody is blamed for failing to act in this way, but those who do earn special merit. The concept of good, like the concept of truth, is an ideal concept. An ideal concept is never matched completely by reality.

The Gospel rightly says: "No one is good except God alone."[39] This means that no human being, but only God, would completely fulfil this ideal concept. A human being can only try to get nearer to God and the ideal of the good.

If the ideal concept of the good cannot be fully realised, so much the less can it be theoretically exhausted by our explanation of the morally good by means of the generalisation rule. Nevertheless, the generalisation rule is a minimum condition that must also be fulfilled by a maximum morality. This rule is a necessary (but by no means sufficient) condition for the maximum morality of loving one's neighbour and one's enemy.

Measured by a conventional minimum morality or *Sittlichkeit*, and even more by the prudential rules of sheer selfishness, this love is unreasonable. Tolstoy's character Levin, for example, says:

> Reason discovered the struggle for existence, and the law that requires us to kill all who hinder the satisfaction of our desires. That is the de-

38 Cf. the parable of the good Samaritan, Luke 10, 35: "And on the morrow when he departed, he took out two pence, and gave them to the host, and said unto him, Take care of him; and whatsoever thou spendest more *(quodcumque supererogaveris)*, when I come again, I will repay thee." Transl. King James Bible.

39 Mark, 10, 18; Luke 18, 19. Quoted by Kant, Groundwork, Section 2, p. 408.

> duction of reason. But the love of one's neighbour reason could never discover, because it's unreasonable.[40]

Levin seems to be using the word "unreasonable" for "imprudent", and "reason" for "prudence". Reason, understood in such terms, is rather instrumental: It contents itself with finding the appropriate means to an end set by the struggle for survival. As we believe today, it does not necessarily follow from the struggle for survival that our opponents must be killed. We can just as well spare them. This is the case with stable or species-preserving evolutionary strategies, in which the opponents exercise restraint in using their deadly weapons. But, as Nietzsche said, in one of his lucid moments: "One has regarded life carelessly, if one has failed to see the hand that – kills with leniency."[41]
Nevertheless, Levin, representing thousands who have done more for others than is customary with conventional minimum morality, can only find in this ideal the missing meaning of life (cf. p. 25-26). This ideal is, admittedly, only a personal and internal aim, whereas the external or objective meaning of my life may remain an open question. Nevertheless, Tolstoy's great novel *Anna Karenina* ends with the simple words:

> But my life now, my whole life apart from anything that can happen to me, every minute of it is no longer meaningless, as it was before, but it has the positive meaning of goodness, which I have the power to put into it.[42]

5. The Generalisation Rule as an Axiomatic Postulate of Practical Reason

We have explained the minimum condition of the good by the conflict of our will that follows from our failure to adhere to it. If an individual were to say "I want to do only what benefits me", we would be able to tell him that he wants something that he will be unable to want as soon as he generalises the subjective principle of his will. For then the others would also be able to do only what is to their advantage, without taking account of his vital interests. But what if he were to ask us: "Why should I generalise the

40 Tolstoy, Anna Karenina, Part 8, Chapter 12. Transl. Constance Black Garnett with modification.
41 Nietzsche, Beyond Good and Evil, Chapter 4, § 69, p. 86. Transl. Zimmern.
42 Tolstoy, Anna Karenina, Part 8, Chapter 19. Transl. Constance Black.

subjective principles of my will if I suffer no disadvantage by not generalising them?"

At this point, we can give him no further explanation. We would only be able to do so by introducing premises that cannot be supported by empirical evidence – such as arguing, for example, that all human beings are numerically one. In this case, the potential conflict between my vital interests and those of others would be overcome. Whatever I would do for the others, I would also do for myself. Whatever the others would do for me, they would also do for themselves. In either case, the rules of prudence would coincide with those of morality.

But the rules of morality are characterised by the fact that they do not always coincide with those of prudence. The moral demands, and the generalisation rule in particular, came into being because we are not all one and because there is a potential conflict between my will and the will of the others. Just as we must accept the metalogical axioms of identity and non-contradiction as institutions of the human language community (cf. pp. 67-69), so, too, must we accept the generalisation rule as an axiomatic meta-institution above the institutional facts of morality. We must accept the metalogical axioms because without them we cannot talk meaningfully. We must accept the meta-institution of the generalisation rule because we want to overcome the potential conflict between my own will and the will of others.

While in relation to the metalogical axioms, sceptics become embroiled in a contradiction (*Widerspruch*) in theoretical reason, in relation to the generalisation rule, they face only a discord (*Widerstreit*) in practical reason or the will. The difference is that a contradiction in theoretical reason is a logical contradiction, while discord in practical reason or the will is a real conflict. This real conflict of having to will something that I do not will can occur at any time. But it usually does not occur until others will something that I do not will. Therefore, its occurrence or non-occurrence depends on empirical conditions.

Since not willing the generalisation rule does not entail a logical contradiction, the generalisation rule cannot be proven in the same way as the metalogical axioms, for instance, by the inconsistency of the attempt to abolish it. Yet, it can also not be proven in the same way as an empirical law by claiming that, as experience teaches us, moral behaviour always pays. On the contrary, honesty may, on occasion, be very costly.

Rather, the generalisation rule itself is a normative axiom for which neither logical nor empirical reasons can be given. It is a *characteristic of* morality that it can make demands on me that go beyond the pursuit of my interests. However, an attempt to explain what goes beyond the pursuit of my interests through those very same interests is predestined to fail. It leaves a gap in the argument, or a stain that cannot be erased. Thus, Mill's proof of utilitarianism starting from the axiom "Everybody strives for happiness, pleasure and utility" leaves a blemish in the picture of classic utilitarianism.

Kant realised that the generalisation rule, or categorical imperative – in his view "the supreme principle of morality" – cannot be explained any further and we can only "comprehend" its "*incomprehensibility*".[43]

Admittedly, we are faced here not with the "incomprehensibility" of a supernatural "fact of reason", but rather with the "incomprehensibility" of a certain form of life. It is a form of life that *wills* this rule, whether implicitly or explicitly.

I am tempted to call this form of life the form of life of human beings *as human beings*. If I were to be asked the question, "Why should I generalise the subjective principles of my behaviour if I incur no disadvantage by not generalising them?", I would only be able to answer, "You should still generalise the subjective principles of your behaviour". And if I were then to be asked the further question, "Why should I will something for which you cannot give me a reason?", I would then only be able to answer (adapting a saying of Wittgenstein's) (cf. p. 40), "Here we can only *describe* and say: moral life is like that".

This has brought us to a provisional ending of our introduction to key concepts of philosophy. Even though we have not yet seen the sun – that is, in the words of Plato, "the Idea of the Good"[44] or supposed "Principle of Everything"[45] we have nevertheless worked our way to some small extent out of the cave. Let us rest here for a while before we continue to move "from here to there"[46] – perhaps to "the end of the journey".[47]

What all of these concepts had in common was that we had assumed them, but had been unable to grasp them completely by means of our elucidations. That was particularly noticeable in connection with the last three concepts: truth, being and good. Their content extended beyond any explicit definition. The key concepts of philosophy are the meanings of key terms of philosophy. The fact that we were unable to elucidate fully the

43 Kant, Groundwork, Section 3, Concluding Remark, p. 463. Transl. Gregor.

44 Plato, R., Book 6, 508 e, Book 7, 517b8-9.

45 Plato, R., Book 6, 511 b.

46 A basic formula frequently used by Plato, Phdr. 250 e, R. 529 a, 619 c, Tht. 176a-b.

47 Plato, R., Book 7, 532 c.

meanings of these key terms shows that they cannot be exhausted by our elucidations. What we have grasped by means of them were only aspects of these concepts as they appeared to us because of the cognitive "weakness of [our] *logoi*",[48] that is, our narratives and arguments.This book was intended as a record of a brief walk through philosophy and I am fully aware of its shortcomings.

The experience of philosophical inadequacy, however, has been expressed in a more joyful way by poet Rainer Maria Rilke. Therefore, at the provisional end of our philosophical walk, let me return to Rilke's poem "The Walk" (cf. p. 27) and reproduce it now in its entirety:

> Fixed on the sunlit hill, my gaze
> runs ahead of the road I have scarcely entered on.
> So does what we were unable to grasp
> grasp us, full of appearance, from the distance –
>
> and transform us, even if we fail to reach it,
> into what, though hardly sensing it, we are:
> a sign waves in reply to our sign ...
> But we feel only the headwind.

48 Plato, Ep. VII 343 a.

Bibliography

First or standard editions and English translations.

Angelleli, I., "The Meaning(s) of "Is": Normative vs. Naturalistic Views of Language" in: A. Koslow, A. Buchsbaum (Eds.), The Road to Universal Logic, Studies in Universal Logic, Cham 2015, 171-179.

Aristotle, *Analytica posteriora* in *Analytica priora et posteriora*, recensuit brevique adnotatione instruxit W. D. Ross, Oxford 1956. Transl. J. Barnes, Posterior Analytics, *Posterior Analytics.* Oxford 1975, 1993² = [Analytica Posteriora].

Aristotle, *De anima*, recognovit brevique adnotatione critica instruxit W. D. Ross, Oxford 1956. Transl. C. D. C. Reeve, Indianapolis = [De an.].

Aristotle, *Categoriae et liber de Interpretatione*, recognovit brevique adnotatione critica instruxit L. Minio-Paluello, Oxford 1949. Transl. John L. Ackrill, *Aristotle's Categories and De interpretation*, Oxford 1969 = [Cat.] / [De int.].

Aristotle, *Ethica Nichomachea*, recognovit brevique adnotatione critica instruxit I. Bywater, Oxford 1894. Transl. W. D. Ross, revised with an Introduction and Notes by Lesley Brown, *Nichomachean Ethics*, Oxford 2009 = [EN].

Aristotle, *Metaphysica*, recognovit brevique adnotatione critica instruxit W. Jaeger, Oxford 1957. Transl. W. D. Ross, Metaphysics, Oxford 2009 = [Metaph.].

Aristotle, *Politica*, recognovit brevique adnotatione critica instruxit W. D. Ross, Oxford 1957 = [Pol.]. Transl. Benjamin Jowett, Politics, New York 2000 = [Pol.].

Aristotle, Protrepticus. An Attempt at Reconstruction by I. Düring in *Studia Graeca et Latina Gothoburgensia,* XII, Göteborg 1961 = [Protrepticus].

Aristotle, *Topica et Sophistici Elenchi*, recensuit brevique adnotatione critica instruxit W. D. Ross, Oxford 1958. Transl. W. A. Pickard, Cambridge, Topics, in Topics, Lawrence 2006 = [Top.].

Augustine, Saint, *Confessions*, 1st ed. Strasbourg before 1470. Quoted from *Confessions, Texte établi et traduit par P. de Labriolle*, I, Paris 5th ed. 1950, II, Paris 3rd ed. 1947. Transl. Henry Chadwick, Confessions, Oxford 1992 = [Conf.].

Ayer, A. J., *Language, Truth and Logic*, London 1936, 2nd ed. 1967.

Beaney, M., *The Frege Reader*, Oxford 1997.

Bernays, P., *Bemerkungen zu Ludwig Wittgensteins "Bemerkungen über die Grundlagen der Mathematik,"* in *Ratio*, 1959, 3, 1-18 = [Bemerkungen]. Transl. Erich Reck, Comments on Ludwig Wittgenstein's Remarks on the foundations of mathematics (1959), Pittsburgh 1959.

Bonola, R., *Die Nichteuklidische Geometrie, Historisch-kritische Darstellung ihrer Entwicklung*, Ed. H. Liebmann, Leipzig/Berlin 1919. Transl. H. C. Carslaw, Non-Euclidean Geometry, Chicago 2010 = [Non-Euclidean Geometry].

Brentano, F., *Psychologie vom empirischen Standpunkt*, Leipzig 1874 (I), Quoted from F. Brentano, *Psychologie vom empirischen Standpunkt*, I, Ed. O. Kraus, Hamburg 1924. Transl. Antos C. Rancurello, D. B. Terrelland, Linda L. McAlister, Psychology from an Empirical Standpoint, London 1973 = [Psychology I].

Brentano, F., *Von der Klassifikation psychischer Phänomene*, in *Psychologie vom empirischen Standpunkt* (II), Leipzig 1911. Quoted from F. Brentano, *Psychologie vom empirischen Standpunkt*, II, Ed. O. Kraus, Hamburg 1925. Transl. Antos C. Rancurello, D. B. Terrelland, Linda L. McAlister, Psychology from an Empirical Standpoint, London 1973 = [Psychology II].

Brunschwig, J., *Revisiting Plato's Cave* in *Proceedings of the Boston Area Colloquium in Ancient Philosophy*, 19, 145-177.

Burkert, W., *Platon oder Pythagoras? Zum Ursprung des Wortes 'Philosophie,'* in *Hermes* 88, 1960, 150-177.

Butler, J., *Fifteen Sermons*, London 1726. Quoted from *The Works of Joseph Butler*, Ed. W. E. Gladstone, II, Sermons, etc., Oxford 1896.

Cantor, G., *Beiträge zur Begründung der transfiniten Mengenlehre*, in *Matheematische Annalen*, 46, 1895, 481-512, 49, 1897, 207-246. Quoted from G. Cantor, *Gesammelte Abhandlungen mathematischen und philosophischen Inhalts*, Ed. F. Zermelo, Berlin 1932, 282-356. Transl. Philip Jourdain, Contributions to the Founding of the Theory of Transfinite Numbers, New York 1915 = [Contributions].

Carnap, R., *Logical Foundations of Probability*, Chicago 1950.

Chisholm, R., *Person and Object*, London/La Salle 1976 = [Person and Object].

Copi, I. M., *Introduction to Logic*, New York/London 1953, 15th ed. 2020 = [Introduction to Logic].

Davidson, D., *James Joyce and Humpty Dumpty* in *Proceedings of the Norwegian Academy of Science and Letters*, 1989, 54-66. Repr. in *D. Davidson, Truth, Language and History*, Oxford 2005, 143-157.

Descartes, R., *Meditationes de prima philosophia*, Paris 1641. Quoted from *Oeuvres de Descartes publiées par Ch. Adam & P. Tannéry, Meditationes de Prima Philosophia*, VII, Paris 1973 = [Meditations]. Transl. J. Cottingham, *Meditations on First Philosophy*, Cambridge 1996 = [Meditations].

Descartes, R., *Principia philosophiae*, Amsterdam 1644. Transl. J. Cottingham, R. Stoothoff and D. Murdoch, *Principles of Philosophy*, in *Selected Philosophical Writings*, Cambridge 1988.

Diels, H., Die Fragmente der Vorsokratiker, Griechisch und deutsch, Berlin 1903, hg. v. W. Kranz, Berlin 1968 = [D/K].

Euclid, *Elementa*, Ed. J.-L. Heiberg and H. Menge, Leipzig 1883-1916 = [Elements]. Transl. D. E. Joyce, *Euclid's Elements*, Worcester MA 1996 = [Elements].

Ferber, R., *Das normative "ist" [das Sein Gottes und die Leibniz-Schellingsche Frage*, in *Zeitschrift für philosophische Forschung*, 42, 1988, 371-396 = [Normative "it", Being of God, Leibniz-Schelling-Question].

Ferber, R., *Das normative "ist" und das konstative "soll"*, in *Archiv für Rechts- und Sozialphilosophie*, 74, 1988, 185-199 = [The normative 'is' and the constative 'ought'].

Ferber, R., *Platos Idee des Guten*, St. Augustin 1984, 2nd rev. ed. St. Augustin 1989, reprint 2015 = [Idea of the Good].

Ferber, R., *Die Unwissenheit des Philosophen oder Warum hat Plato die ungeschriebene Lehre nicht geschrieben?*, St. Augustin 1991, 2nd rev. ed. *Warum hat Platon die ungeschriebene Lehre nicht geschrieben?*, Munich 2007.

Ferber, R., *"Lebensform" oder "Lebensformen" – Zwei Addenda zur Kontroverse zwischen N. Garver und R. Haller* in *Akten des 15. Internationalen Wittgenstein-Symposiums*, part 2, Ed. K. Puhl, Vienna 1993, 270-276 = [Form of life or forms of life].

Ferber, R., *Moralische Urteile als Beschreibungen institutioneller Tatsachen. Unterwegs zu einer neuen Theorie moralischer Urteile*, in *Archiv für Rechts- und Sozialphilosophie*, 79, 1993, 372-392. Partial English translation, *Moral Judgments as Descriptions of Institutional Facts*, in *Analyomen* 1, Berlin, New York 1994, 719-729 = [Moral Judgments].

Ferber, R., *Für eine propädeutische Lektüre des "Politicus"* in *Reading the Statesman, Proceedings of the III Symposium Platonicum, International Plato Studies*, 4, Ed. Ch. Rowe, St Augustin 1995, 63-74. Partial English translation in: "The absolute Good and the human goods", in: Giovanni Reale and Samuel Scolnicov (Eds.) 2002, *New Images of Plato: Dialogues on the Idea of the Good*, Academia Verlag, Sankt Augustin, 187-196, Repr. in Ferber, 2020, 197-214 = [Propedeutic Lecture of the *Politicus*].

Ferber, R., *Why did Plato maintain the theory of ideas in the "Timaeus"?*, in *Interpreting the Timaeus and Critias, Proceedings of the IV Symposium Platonicum, International Plato Studies 9*, Ed. T. Calvo/L. Brisson, St. Augustin 1997, 179-186. Enlarged German version in Ferber, 2020, 2015-237 = [Theory of ideas in "Timaeus"].

Ferber, R., *Die "metaphysische Perle" im "Sumpf der Tropen": Einige Bemerkungen zur aristotelischen Metaphysik, Z 17, 1041 b 4-9.* In: Lazzari A., Metamorphosen der Vernunft: Festschrift für Karen Gloy. Würzburg 2003, 63-82. Repr. in Ferber, 2020, 273-293 = [Metaphysische Perle].

Ferber, R., *"Ho de diôkei men hapasa psychê kai toutou heneka panta prattei"* in: *Dialogues on Plato's Politeia (Republic). Selected Papers from the Ninth Symposium Platonicum*, Ed. N. Notomi /L. Brisson, International Plato Studies, 31, Sankt Augustin 2013, 233-241. Enlarged German version in Ferber, 2020, 93-113 = [Ho de diôkei].

Ferber, R., *Platonische Aufsätze* in Beiträge zur Altertumskunde, vol. 386, Berlin / Boston 2020.

Feyerabend, P., *Problems of Empiricism*, *Philosophical Papers*, 2. Cambridge 1981 = [Problems of Empiricism].

Frege, G., *Begriffsschrift, eine der arithmetischen nachgebildete Formelsprache des reinen Denkens*, Halle 1879. Quoted from *Begriffsschrift und andere Aufsätze*, 2nd ed. by I. Angelelli, Darmstadt 1973. Transl. S. Bauer-Mengelberg, *Concept Script*, in Jean Van Heijenoort (Ed.), From Frege to Gödel, Cambridge, MA 1967 = [Begriffsschrift].

Frege, G., *Die Grundlagen der Arithmetik. Eine logisch-mathematische Untersuchung über den Begriff der Zahl*, Breslau 1884. Quoted from reprint by Wissenschaftliche Buchgesellschaft, Darmstadt 1961 of reprint Breslau 1934 = [Foundations of Arithmetic]. Transl. J. L. Austin, *The Foundations of Arithmetic: A logico-mathematical enquiry into the concept of number*, by J. L. Austin, Oxford 2nd ed. 1974.

Frege, G., *Über Sinn und Bedeutung*, in *Zeitschrift für Philosophie und philosophische Kritik*, 100, 1892, 23-50. Quoted from *Gottlob Frege: Kleine Schriften*, Ed. I. Angelelli, Hildesheim 1967, 43-162 = [Sinn and Bedeutung]. Transl. M. Black, On *Sinn* and *Bedeutung*, in Ed. Beaney M., The Frege Reader, Oxford 1997, 151-180.

Frege, G., *Begriff und Gegenstand*, in *Vierteljahresschrift für wissenschaftliche Philosophie,* 16, 1892. Quoted from *Gottlob Frege: Kleine Scriften*, Ed. I. Angelelli, Hildesheim 1967, 167-178. Transl. P. Geach and M. Black, Concept and Object, in Ed. Beaney M., The Frege Reader, Oxford 1997, 181-193 = [Concept and Object].

Frege, G., *Über die Grundlagen der Geometrie*, in *Jahresbericht der Deutschen Mathematiker-Vereinigung*, 12, 1903, 319-324. Quoted from *Gottlob Frege: Kleine Schriften*, Ed. I. Angelelli, Hildesheim 1967, 262-266. Transl. Eike-Henner W. Kluge, On the foundations of geometry: Second series, in Collected Papers on Mathematics, Logic, and Philosophy, Ed. B. McGuiness, Oxford 1984 = [Foundations of Geometry].

Frege, G., *Unbekannte Briefe Freges über die Grundlagen der Geometrie und Antwortbrief Hilberts an Frege*, in *Sitzungsberichte der Heidelberger Akademie der Wissenschaften,* Mathematisch-Naturwissenschaftliche Klasse, 2, Heidelberg 1941, 3-31 = [Letters].

Frege, G., *Der Gedanke. Eine logische Untersuchung,* in *Beiträge zur Philo-sophie des deutschen Idealismus,* I, 1918/1919, 58-77. Quoted from *Gottlob Frege: Kleine Schriften*, Ed. I. Angelelli, Hildesheim 1967, 343-362 = [Thought]. Transl. P. T. Geach and R. H. Stoothoff, Thought, in Ed. Beaney M., The Frege Reader, Oxford 1997, 325-345.

Frege, G., *Logik*, in *Nachgelassene Schriften und Wissenschaftlicher Briefwechsel*, Ed. H. Hermes et al., Hamburg 1969, 137-163 = [Logic]. Transl. P. Long and R. M. White, *Logic*, in *Posthumous Writings*, Oxford 1979, 126-151, Extract in Beaney, 227-250.

Frege, G., *Logik in der Mathematik*, in *Nachgelassene Schriften und Wissenschaftlicher Briefwechsel*, Ed. H. Hermes et al., Hamburg 1969, 219-270. Transl. P. Long and R. M. White, *Logic in Mathematics*, in *Posthumous Writings*, Oxford 1979, 203-250 = [Logic in Mathematics].

Freud, S., *Die Traumdeutung*, Leipzig/Vienna 1900. Quoted from *Gesammelte Werke*, II/3, Frankfurt 1942. Transl. A. A. Brill, The Interpretation of Dreams, New York 1913 = [Interpretation of Dreams].

Goodman, N., *Fact, Fiction and Forecast*, Cambridge, MA 1955.

Grice, P., *Meaning* in *The Philosophical Review*, 55, 1957, 377-388.

Habermas, J., *Wahrheitstheorien* in *Wirklichkeit und Reflexion*, Ed. H. Fahrenbach, Pfullingen 1972, 211-265 = [Wahrheitstheorien].

Habermas, J., *Die Neue Unübersichtlichkeit. Kleine Politische Schriften*, V, Frankfurt 1983 = [New Obscurity]. Transl. Shierry Weber Nicholsen, The New Conservatism: Cultural Criticism and the Historians' Debate, Oxford 1990 = [New Obscurity].

Hare, R. M., *The Language of Morals*, Oxford 1952.

Hegel, G. W. F., *Vorlesungen über die Geschichte der Philosophie*, I, Berlin 1833-1836. *Werke,* Ed. E. Moldenhauer and K. M. Michel, Frankfurt a. M. 1971, based on *Werke*, 1832-1843. Transl. E. S. Haldane, Lectures on the History of Philosophy v. 1, Lincoln, NE 1995 = [History of Philosophy].

Hegel, G. W. F., Grundlinien der Philosophie des Rechts oder Naturrecht und Staatswissenschaft im Grundrisse, Berlin 1821. Quoted from the edition of *Werke,* Ed. E. Moldenhauer and K. M. Michel, Frankfurt a. M. 1971, based on *Werke*, 1832-1843 Transl. Nisbet, Cambridge 1991 = [Philosophy of Right].

Heidegger, M., *Sein und Zeit*, Halle 1927 = [BaT]. Transl. John Macquarrie and Edward Robinson, *Being and Time*, New York 1962 = [BaT].

Heidegger, M., *Was ist Metaphysik*, Bonn 1929. Quoted from enlarged the 6th ed. Frankfurt a. M. = [Metaphysics]. Transl. David Ferrall Krell, *What is Metaphysics*, in *Basic Writings*, London 1978 = [Metaphysics].

Hilbert, D., *Grundlagen der Geometrie*, Leipzig 1899. Transl. Leo Unger, *Foundations of Geometry*, Chicago 1971.

Holenstein, E., *Sprachliche Universalien. Eine Untersuchung zur Natur des menschlichen Geistes*, Bochum 1985 = [Sprachliche Universalien].

Horwich, P., *Truth*, Oxford 1990 = [Truth].

Hume, D., *A Treatise of Human Nature, Being an Attempt to Introduce the Experimental Method of Reasoning into Moral Subjects*, London 1739-40. Quoted from edition by L. A. Selby-Bigge, Oxford 1888, 2nd rev. ed. P. H. Nidditch, Oxford 1978 = [Treatise].

Hume, D., *An Enquiry Concerning Human Understanding*, London 1748. Quoted from *Enquiries Concerning the Human Understanding and Concerning the Principles of Morals by David Hume*, reprint of posthumous ed. of 1777, Ed. L. A. Selby-Bigge, Oxford 1888 = [Enquiry].

James, W., *Pragmatism. A New Name for Some Old Ways of Thinking. Popular Lectures on Philosophy*, London 1907 = [Pragmatism].

Kant, I., *Kritik der reinen Vernunft*, Riga 1781. Transl. Paul Guyer and Allen W. Wood, Critique of Pure Reason, Cambridge 1998 = [CPR].

Kant, I., *Prolegomena zu einer jeden künftigen Metaphysik, die als Wissenschaft wird auftreten können*, Riga 1783.

Kant, I., *Grundlegung zur Metaphysik der Sitten*, Riga 1785. Transl. Mary Gregor, Groundwork of the Metaphysic of Morals, Cambridge 1998 = [Groundwork].

Kant, I., Kritik der praktischen Vernunft, Riga 1788. Transl. Gregor, *Critique of Practical Reason*, Cambridge 1996 = [CPrR].

Kant, I., *Anthropologie in pragmatischer Hinsicht*. Königsberg 1798 = [Anthropology]. Transl. R. B. Loudon, *Anthropology from a Pragmatic Point of View*, Cambridge 2006 = [Anthropology].

Kant, I., *Bemerkungen zu den Beobachtungen über das Gefühl des Schönen und Erhabenen*, in *Kant's Gesammelte Schriften*, ed. by Preußische Akademie der Wissenschaften, 20, 3. Abt., Handschriftlicher Nachlaß, 7. Band, Berlin 1942. Transl. P, Frierson / P. Guyer, "Remarks in the *Observations on the Feelings of the Beautiful and Sublime" in* "Observations on the Feeling of the Beautiful and Sublime and Other Writings", Cambridge 2011, 65-202 = [Remarks].

Kleve, K., *Did Socrates Exist?*, in: *Grazer Beiträge: Zeitschrift für die klassische Altertumswissenschaft*, 14, 1987, 123-137.

Kripke, S., *Wittgenstein on Rules and Private Language. An Elementary Exposition*, London 1982 = [Wittgenstein on Rules].

Kuhn, T. S., *The Structure of Scientific Revolution*, Chicago 1962 = [Structure].

Leibniz, G. W., *Monadologie*, Jena 1720. Quoted from *Principes de la nature et de la Grace, fondées en Raison – Principes de la Philosophie ou Monadologie*, Ed. A. Robinet, Paris 1954. Transl. R. Arlew and D. Garber, *Monadology*, in *Philosophical Essays*, Indianapolis 1989, 213-224 = [Monadology].

Lichtenberg, G. C., *Aphorismen. Schriften. Briefe*, Ed. W. Promies, Munich 1974 = [Aphorisms]. Transl. R. J. Hollingdale, New York 2000.

Locke, J., *An Essay Concerning Human Understanding*, London 1960. Quoted from 5th enlarged ed., London 1706 = [Essay Concerning Human Understanding].

MacCormick, D. N./Weinberger, O., *An Institutional Theory of Law. New Approaches to Legal Positivism,* Dordrecht et al. 1986 = [Institutional Theory of Law].

Machiavelli, N., *Il Principe*, Rome 1532. Transl. W. K. Marriott, The Prince, London, Toronto, New York 1920.

Mill, J. S., *On Liberty*, London 1859. Quoted after the 2nd ed., London 1863.

Mill, J. S., *Utilitarianism*, London 1861/63, 15th ed., London 1907 = [Utilitarianism].

Moore, G. E., *Principia Ethica*, Cambridge 1903 = [PE].

Moore, G. E., *The Refutation of Idealism* in *Mind* 12, 1903, 433-453.

Morris, C., *Signs, Language and Behavior*, New York 1946 = [Signs, Language, Behaviour].

Nagel, T., *What is it Like to Be a Bat?* in *Philosophical Review*, 83, 1974, 435-450.

Neurath, O., *Protokollsätze*, in *Erkenntnis*, 3, 1932/33, 204-214. Transl. G. Schick, *Protocol Sentences*, in A. J. Ayer Ed., *Logical Positivism*, New York 1959.

Nietzsche, F., *Also sprach Zarathustra. Ein Buch für Alle und Keinen*, Chemnitz 1883 (1. und 2. Teil), Chemnitz 1884 (3. Teil), Leipzig 1885 (4. Teil). Transl. R. J. Hollingdale, *Thus Spoke Zarathustra*, Harmondsworth 1961.

Nietzsche, F., *Jenseits von Gut und Böse. Vorspiel einer Philosophie der Zukunft*, Leipzig 1886. Quoted from *Nietzsche Werke*, Ed. G. Colli and M. Montinari, VI/2, 1-255, Berlin 1968 = [Beyond Good and Evil]. Transl. Helen Zimmern, Beyond Good and Evil, Teddington 2006.

Nietzsche, F., *Zur Genealogie der Moral. Eine Streitschrift*, Leipzig 1887. Quoted from *Nietzsche Werke*, Ed. G. Colli and M. Montinari, VI/2, 259-430, Berlin 1968 = [Genealogy]. Transl. W. Kaufman and R. J. Hollingdale, *On the Genealogy of Morals*, New York 1967.

Ogden, C. K./Richards, I. A., *The Meaning of Meaning. A Study of the Influence of Language upon Thought and the Science of Symbolism*, London 1923 = [Meaning of Meaning].

Ortega y Gasset, Miseria y Esplendor de la Traduccion, Buenos Aires, Nacion, 1937, *Obras completas*, 5, Madrid, Alianza 1983, 431-452. No English translation.

Owen, G. E. L., 1960, 'Logic and Metaphysics in Some Earlier Works of Aristotle,' in I. Düring and G. E. L. Owen (Eds.), *Plato and Aristotle in the Mid-Fourth Century*, Göteborg 1960, 163-190.

Peirce, C., *Collected Papers of Charles Sanders Peirce*, V, *Pragmatism and Pragmaticism*, Cambridge, MA 1963 = [Pragmatism and Pragmaticism].

Peirce, C., *Charles S. Peirce's Letters to Lady Welby*, Ed. I. C. Lieb, New Haven 1953 = [Letters to Lady Welby].

Perry, R. B., *Review of G. E. Moore, The Refutation of Idealism* in *The Journal of Philosophy, Psychology, and Scientific Methods*, 1, 1904, 4 February, 66-67.

Plato, *Apologia Sokratous* in *Platonis Opera*, I, Tetralogias I-II continens, recognoverunt brevique adnotatione critica instruxerunt E. A. Duke, W. F. Hicken, W. D. M. Nicoll, D. B. Robinson, J. C. G. Strachan, Oxford 1995. = [Ap.]. Translations of Plato are my own where not otherwise indicated.

Plato, *Charmides* in *Platonis Opera*, recognovit brevique adnotatione critica instruxit I. Burnet, III, Tetralogias V-VII continens, Oxford 1901 = [Chrm.]

Plato, *Gorgias* in *Platonis Opera*, III, Tetralogias V-VII continens, Oxford 1901 = [Grg.].

Plato, *Kratylos* in *Platonis Opera*, I, Tetralogias I-II continens, Oxford 1901 = [Cra.].

Plato, *Menon* in *Platonis Opera*, III, Tetralogias V-VII continens, Oxford 1901 = [Men.].

Plato, *Phaidon* in *Platonis Opera*, I, Tetralogias I-II continens, Oxford 1996 = [Phd.].

Plato, *Platonis* Republicam recognovit brevique adnotatione critica instruxit S.R. Slings, Oxford 2003 = [R.].

Plato, *Phaidros* in *Platonis Opera*, I, Tetralogias I-II continens, Oxford 1901 = [Phdr.].

Plato, *Philebus* in *Platonis Opera*, II, Tetralogias I-II continens, Oxford 1901 = [Phlb.].

Plato, *Parmenides* in *Platonis Opera*, II, Tetralogias I-II continens, Oxford 1901 = [Prm.].

Plato, *Politikos* in *Platonis Opera*, I, Tetralogias I-II continens, Oxford 1995 = [Plt.].

Plato, *Theaitetos* in *Platonis Opera*, I, Tetralogias I-II continens, Oxford 1995 = [Tht.]. English translation by M. J. Levett, rev. by M. Burnyeat in: Burneat M. The Theaetetus of Plato, Indianapolis / Cambridge 1990.

Plato, *Timaios* in *Platonis Opera*, IV, Tetralogiam VIII continens, Oxford 1902 = [Ti.].

Plato, *Seventh Letter* in *Platonis Opera*, V, Tertralogiam IX, definitiones et spuria continens, Oxford 1907 = [Ep. VII].

Popper, K., *Logik der Forschung*, Vienna 1934. Quoted from the 8th enlarged ed., Tübingen 1984 = [LSD]. Transl. Popper et al., *The Logic of Scientific Discovery*, London 1959.

Popper, K., *Conjectures and Refutations. The Growth of Scientific Knowledge*, London 1963. Quoted from 2002 ed. = [Conjectures and Refutations].

Popper, K., *Objective Knowledge. An Evolutionary Approach*, Oxford 1972 = [Objective Knowledge].

Popper, K., *Auf der Suche nach einer besseren Welt. Vorträge und Aufsätze aus dreißig Jahren*, Munich/Zurich 1984. Transl. Laura J. Bennett, *In Search of a Better World, Lectures and Essays from Thirty Years*, London 1994 = [Better World].

Porphyrios, *Isagoge et in Aristotelis Categorias Commentarium*, Ed. A. Busse, in *Commentaria in Aristotelem Graeca*, IV, 1, Berlin 1887, 1-22. Transl. Edghill = [Introduction].

Putnam, H., *Reason, Truth and History*, Cambridge 1981 = [Reason, Truth and History].

Putnam, H., *Reference and Understanding* in *Meaning and the Moral Sciences*, London 1978, 97-122.

Quine, W. V. O., *Word and Object*, Cambridge, MA 1960 = [Word and Object].

Quine, W. V. O., *Ontological Relativity and Other Essays*, New York/London 1969 = [Ontological Relativity].

Quine, W. V. O., *Quiddities, An Intermittently Philosophical Dictionary*, Cambridge, MA 1987 = [Quiddities].

Quine, W. V. O., *Pursuit of Truth*, Cambridge, MA/London 1990 = [Pursuit of Truth].

Quine, W. V. O., *From Stimulus to Science*, Cambridge, MA/London 1995 = [From Stimulus to Science].

Ramsey, F. P., *Facts and Propositions* in *Proceedings of the Aristotelian Society*, Suppl. Vol. 7, 1927, 153-170 = [Facts and Propositions].

Reichenbach, H., *The Theory of Probability. An Inquiry into the Logical and Mathematical Foundation of the Calculus of Probability*, Berkeley/Los Angeles 1949 = [Probability].

Rorty, R., Philosophy and the Mirror of Nature, Oxford 1980 = [Mirror of Nature].

Russell, B., *The Problems of Philosophy*, London et al. 1912 = [Problems].

Russell, B., See also under Whitehead, A. N.

Salmon, W. C., *Hans Reichenbach's vindication of induction* in *Erkenntnis*, 33, 1991, 99-122.

Saint-John Perse, *Allocution au Banquet Nobel du 10 décembre 1960*, in *Oeuvres complètes*, Paris 1972, 443-447. Transl. W. H. Auden, Speech of acceptance upon the award of the Nobel Prize for Literature delivered in Stockholm December 10, 1960, New York 1961.

Schopenhauer, A., *Über die vierfache Wurzel des Satzes vom hinreichenden Grunde. Eine philosophische Abhandlung*, Rudolfstadt 1813. Quoted from *Arthur Schopenhauer's sämmtliche Werke*, Ed. J. Frauenstädt, 2nd ed., I, Leipzig 1916 = [Fourfold Root]. Transl. Mme. K. Hillebrand, *On the Fourfold Root of the Principle of Sufficient Reason*, New York 2007.

Schopenhauer, A., *Die Welt als Wille und Vorstellung*, II, Leipzig 1844. Quoted from *Arthur Schopenhauer's sämmtliche Werke*, Ed. J. Frauenstädt, 2nd ed., III, Leipzig 1916 = [W II]. Transl. R. B. Haldane and J. Kemp, The World as Will and Idea, London 1909.

Searle, J. R., *Speech Acts. An Essay in the Philosophy of Language*, Cambridge 1969 = [Speech Acts].

Searle, J. R., *Making the Social World. The Structure of Human Civilization*, Oxford 2010 = [Making the Social World].

Sextus Empiricus, *Adversus Mathematicos*, VII-XI, Ed. H. Mutschmann, Leipzig 1914 = [M].

Spengler, O., *Der Untergang des Abendlandes. Umrisse einer Morphologie der Weltgeschichte*, Vienna 1918 (vol. I) Munich 1922 (vol. II). Quoted from DTV edition by A. M. Koktanek, Munich 1972. Transl. Charles Francis Atkinson, The Decline of the West, London 1932 = [DW].

Spengler, O., Urfragen. Fragmente aus dem Nachlass. Unter Mitwirkung von M. Schröter, hg. v. A. M. Koktanek, Munich 1965 [Urfragen].

Spinoza, B. de, Metaphysical Thoughts in: *The Collected Works of Spinoza*, vol. 1, Princeton 1985.

Stoicorum veterum fragmenta, Coll. I. ab Arnim, 4 vol. Leipzig 1903 = [SVF].

Tarski, A., *Der Wahrheitsbegriff in den formalisierten Sprachen*, in *Studia Philosophica*, 1, 1933, 261-405. Transl. J. H. Woodger, *The Concept of Truth in Formalised Languages* in *Logic, Semantics, Metamathematics: Papers from 1923 to 1938*, Oxford 1956, 2nd ed. [with the same pagination] and introd. by J. Corcoran, Indianapolis 1983 = [Concept of Truth].

Tarski, A., *The Semantic Conception of Truth and the Foundation of Semantics*, in *Philosophy and Phenomenological Research*, 4, 1944, 341-375 = [Semantic Conception of Truth].

Taylor, A. E., *David Hume and the Miraculous*, in *Philosophical Studies*, London 1934, 330-365 = [Hume and the Miraculous].

Watkins, J., *Science and Scepticism*, Princeton 1984 = [Science and Scepticism].

Weinberger, O., see under MacCormick, D. N.

Whitehead, A. N./Russell, B., *Principia Mathematica*, I, Cambridge et al. 1910. Quoted from 2nd ed. 1927 = [PM].

Wittgenstein, L., *Tractatus logico-philosophicus/Logisch-Philosophische Abhandlung*, in *Annalen der Naturphilosophie* Ed. W. Ostwald, 14, 1921. Quoted from L. Wittgenstein: *Schriften 1*, 9-83, Frankfurt a. M. 1969. Transl. C. K. Ogden, *Tractatus logico-philosophicus*, London 1922 = [TLP].

Wittgenstein, L., *Philosophische Untersuchungen*, in L. Wittgenstein: *Schriften 1*, 279-544, Frankfurt a. M. 1969. Transl. G. E. M. Anscombe, P. M. S. Hacker and J. Schulte, *Philosophical Investigations*, 4th ed. Chichester 2009 = [PI].

Wittgenstein, L., *Philosophische Grammatik, Teil 1, Satz, Sinn des Satzes, Teil 2, Über Logik und Mathematik*, Ed. R. Rhees, Oxford 1969. Quoted from L. Wittgenstein: *Schriften 4*, Frankfurt a.M. 1969. Transl. A. Kenny, *Philosophical Grammar*, Oxford 1974 = [PG].

Wittgenstein, L., *Letzte Schriften über die Philosophie der Psychologie*, Ed. G. E. M. Anscombe, London 1984. Transl. C. G. Luckhardt and Maximilian A. E. Aue, *Last Writings on the Philosophy of Psychology*, Oxford 1992 = [LW].

Wittgenstein, L., *Remarks on the Foundations of Mathematics*, Ed. G. H. v. Wright, R. Rhees, G. E. M. Anscombe, Transl. Anscombe, Oxford 1956, 2nd rev. ed., 1978 = [RFM].

Wittgenstein, L., *Bemerkungen über Frazers Golden Bough*, in *Synthese*, 17, 1967, 233-253. Transl. A. C. Miles, Remarks on Frazer's *Golden Bough*, Retford 1983 = [RFGB].

Wright, G. H. v., *The Logic of Preference. An Essay*, Edinburgh 1963 = [Logic of Preference].

Name Index

Subject Index (Selection)

Zeitfracht Medien GmbH
Ferdinand-Jühlke-Straße 7
99095 Erfurt, Deutschland
produktsicherheit@kolibri360.de